TWO CENTURIES
of
ROYAL WEDDINGS

TWO CENTURIES
of
ROYAL WEDDINGS

Christopher Warwick

Foreword by
Elizabeth Longford

Arthur Barker Limited London
A subsidiary of Weidenfeld (Publishers) Limited

Published in Great Britain by Arthur Barker Limited
91 Clapham High Street, London SW4 7TA

ISBN 0 213 16739 5
Printed in Great Britain by
Butler & Tanner Ltd, Frome and London

Picture research by Caroline Lucas

Contents

Acknowledgements

I would first like to acknowledge the gracious permission of Her Majesty the Queen for excerpts from speeches and personal correspondence quoted in this book. I received the kind co-operation of members of the various Royal Households, and would particularly like to acknowledge the invaluable assistance of Mrs Anne Wall, Miss Mona Mitchell and Miss Frances Dimond. I owe a very great debt to the Countess of Longford, not only for her continuing interest in this project and for agreeing so readily to contribute a foreword, but also for her wise counsel. Among the people who gave me assistance over the research of the book I would like to thank Sir Marcus Worsley, Bt; Mr Reginald Pullen, Receiver-General of Westminster Abbey; the late Sir Norman Hartnell; Mrs Maureen Baker; Mr John Cavanagh; Mr Tom Hustler; Miss Jane Bartlett; Mrs Alison Warington-Smyth and Mr Anthony J. Camp.

Hugo Vickers put a great deal of material at my disposal, and Audrey Russell outlined some of the complexities of broadcasting; to them both I would like to express my deep appreciation. Finally, I would like to offer my gratitude and heartfelt thanks to Brian Auld, Sara Paul, Tom and Annabel Jenkins for their encouragement at all times; to Simon Dally for giving me the opportunity of writing this book; to Marcia Fenwick for her patience and editorial expertise; and to Alex MacCormick and Linda Osband for their tolerance and words of wisdom.

C.W.

Illustrations

Illustrations in this book are reproduced by kind permission of the following:

By gracious permission of HM the Queen: 5 *above*, 9, 15 *above*, 25, 27, 29 *below*, 33, 35 *below*, 37 *above*, 39, 41 *below*, 44 *below*, 45, 49, 52, 53, 57, 75 *above*; Camera Press; *frontispiece*, 59, 67, 73, 83, 93 *below*, 95, 101, 130 *below*, 137, 139, 141; *Daily Express*: 129 *above*; *Daily Telegraph*: 123, 130 *above*; *Illustrated London News*: 24, 63; Keystone Press: 5 *below*, 7, 69, 71 *above*, 85, 87, 93 *above*, 104, 105, 110–11, 115, 117, 126–7, 129 *below*, 133; Mansell Collection: 17, 29 *above*; Mary Evans Picture Library: 13, 15 *below*; National Monuments Record: 3, 11 *below*; Radio Times Hulton Picture Library: 35 *above*, 37 *below*, 41 *above*, 44 *above*, 71 *below*, 75 *below*; Victoria and Albert Museum: 11 *above*.

The author and publisher have taken all possible care to trace and acknowledge the ownership of all illustrations. If by chance an incorrect attribution has been made we will be happy to correct it in any future reprint, provided that we receive notification.

Foreword
by Elizabeth Longford

Most people would agree that there is something magical about the monarchy, though few would be able to say exactly what it is. Although the author of this colourful historical narrative feels the romance of the Crown, he realizes it is not his task to analyse it. His aim is to deploy one aspect of that magic before our eyes, in a form that from time immemorial has seemed particularly glamorous – the Royal Wedding. It is for us to watch the royal spectacle unfold in these pages and then ask ourselves, if we wish, wherein lies its secret.

Over a hundred years ago, the famous constitutional writer, Walter Bagehot, noted the rôle played by royal weddings in the build-up of the Crown's position. 'A princely marriage', he wrote, 'is the brilliant edition of a universal fact' – brilliant, because a princely marriage is compact of pageantry; universal, because marriage is a common human experience – 'and as such', added Bagehot, 'it rivets mankind'.

Christopher Warwick gives due weight to the splendour, solemnity and tradition embodied in these occasions. As a young writer, he is also impressed by the gradual changes that have taken place. His accurate and wide research demonstrates how some traditions are preserved while others are dropped in accordance with modern needs. The greatest change of all lies towards more informality. Our interest today focuses as much on the individuals involved, with all their human traits, as on their exalted rank. In Christopher Warwick's words: 'My research became even more fascinating when I decided *not* to look upon the various royalties mentioned in these pages as kings and queens, dukes and duchesses, princes and princesses but simply as parents, grandparents, brothers, sisters, aunts, uncles and cousins.'

His researches have nonetheless led him into many interesting discoveries that are specifically royal. It was because the bride was a *princess* that a BBC commentator thought it worth while to sway perilously in a 'flying coffin' above the heads of the congregation. It is because *royal* schedules are so tight that the Registrar of Westminster Abbey has to collect some of the signatures at the wedding-breakfast, instead of in the Chapel of St Edward the Confessor.

This book brings out the rich variety rather than uniformity even in royal weddings. How do the brides dispose of their bouquets, for instance? Some are laid on the tomb of the Unknown Warrior in Westminster Abbey *after* the service, other flowers have found their way on to the Cenotaph, while the bouquet of Lady Elizabeth Bowes-Lyon was laid on the Unknown Warrior's tomb *before* the service began. No uniformity appears in methods of transport: it can be a coach, carriage, landau or Rolls-Royce; though one may safely guess that when Prince Charles is married at the Abbey he will ride in the Glass Coach.

Today we take the Abbey for granted as the properly magnificent setting for royal weddings. That, however, has not always been the case. Every king and queen of England has been crowned there since William the Conqueror; but by no means every sovereign has been married there, far less every prince or princess of the royal house. In our own day we can point to the future George VI, his daughters the Princesses Elizabeth and Margaret, and his granddaughter Princess Anne, all being married in the Abbey. In the past we can name Henry I and Richard III. The fact remains that the historic 'locale' (as Queen Victoria called it) for a royal wedding was as varied as Greenwich, the Queen's Chapel in Whitehall, and Kew. Queen Anne, Queen Charlotte and Queen Victoria were all married in the Chapel Royal, St James's, a 'schocking locale' according to the young Victoria, apparently because the choir always sang 'schockingly'. Her predecessors were married in the late evening, she in broad daylight. Perhaps it was fortunate for the future George IV that royal weddings were traditionally solemnized at night. The candle-light must have done something to conceal the fact that he was drunk, the only condition in which he could face his abhorred bride, Caroline of Brunswick.

There is little doubt that Queen Victoria would have preferred something more like a secret wedding for herself. Shy by nature, she hated publicity and suggested a room in Buckingham Palace for her marriage ceremony with Prince Albert; but Lord Melbourne, her Prime Minister, forbade it. She reverted to semi-secrecy at the wedding of her eldest son, the Prince of Wales, in St George's Chapel, Windsor. In deepest mourning for her beloved Albert, she hid herself away in Queen Catherine of Aragon's closet, where she could see without being seen, except by the very inquisitive.

When we reach the period of which Christopher Warwick mainly writes, the wheel has come full circle. The publicity and size of royal weddings would have made Queen Victoria 'gasp and stretch' her already prominent eyes. But the relaxed atmosphere which was so often absent in her day has, paradoxically, returned with the less private wedding. Even a huge abbey wedding can seem 'natural' and informal; particularly if the bride's father is a wit and can make her smile just as she starts up the aisle with the whispered aside, 'It's not too late to change your mind!'

A marriage begins by joining man and wife
together, but this relationship between two people,
however deep at the time, needs to develop and
mature with the passing years. For that it must be
held firm in the web of family relationships
between parents and children, between
grandparents and grandchildren, between cousins,
aunts and uncles.

From a speech made by Her Majesty Queen Elizabeth II on
20 November 1972 to celebrate her Silver Wedding Anniversary.

ix

1
Arranging a Royal Wedding

As might be expected, the factors that have to be borne in mind by those responsible for arranging a royal wedding are legion. That such an occasion can be organized, often in as little as three months, says a good deal for the skills of those directly concerned. The difference between a royal wedding and one that takes place in a local church is the splendour of the pageantry and, as in the case of the Queen and Prince Philip, the historical significance of the day.

Royal weddings are, admittedly, few in number – there have only been five at Westminster Abbey since the Queen was married there in 1947. State visits and the opening of Parliament are more frequent occurrences, but the one thing all these events have in common is a basic plan laid down long ago to cater for the requirements of royal ceremonial on a grand scale.

In terms of hard cash it is considered indelicate to pry into the cost of a royal wedding, but one thing is quite certain: it is an expensive business. As things stand, the only cost to the taxpayer is in overtime for the police, any specially constructed stands that the Department of the Environment may choose to erect (though for public and press the cost is recovered from the occupants) and any transportation needed for the troops on ceremonial duty. Such payments come out of the small contribution – a few pence per week – each working Briton makes towards the upkeep of the monarchy. For example, when Princess Alexandra was married in 1963, the cost to the country was estimated to have been somewhere in the region of £600.

When Princess Anne got married in 1973, the Queen followed the general pattern of signing a personal cheque to cover the cost of such things as a trousseau, her daughter's wedding-gown included, the flowers, the wedding-breakfast, the invitations and so on.

But there is also money to be made. The Westminster Abbey choir is composed of twelve men and twenty-two boys. For something like a royal marriage, it is likely that other boys from the choirs of the Chapels Royal will be brought in to swell the numbers. The adult choristers, however, are all professional musicians who are contracted by the abbey to attend a certain number of services each year. Where something like a royal wedding is concerned, the musicians invariably earn more than their agreed fee by virtue of their membership of Equity, the actors' union, which entitles them to obtain repeat fees on such things as television broadcasts and radio recordings. It was said that through the wedding of Princess Anne each adult member of the choir that day earned between £200 and £250.

Souvenirs are also big business for a wide variety of companies (commemorative china in particular being sought after as collectors' items). The proceeds from the sale of the *official* wedding programmes have always gone to King George's Jubilee Trust, set up in 1935 following George v's Silver Jubilee.

More immediately relevant to the Royal Family are the arrangements that need to be made to prevent any hitches in the smooth running of what are, after all, important family occasions. Therefore, overall charge is always taken by the Lord Chamberlain, the most senior member of the Royal Household. From his department, located at St James's Palace, the Lord Chamberlain will stage-manage the entire event from start to finish. Included in his numerous responsibilities will be the submission of a provisional guest list to the sovereign, the final despatch of all invitations and the seating arrangements in the body of Westminster Abbey.

To the Master of the Household falls the duty of organizing the wedding-breakfast and the supervision and direction of all domestic arrangements within Buckingham Palace. After discussions, the sovereign's personal florist will make the necessary arrangements for floral decorations, though not, it should be said, so far as Westminster Abbey is concerned: she is purely responsible for flower arrangements within the Queen's own residences, using blooms grown at Windsor as a rule, though for a banquet or a wedding she will buy wholesale stock from Covent Garden to supplement what is already to hand. At the abbey, the Receiver-General supervises the distribution of flowers, once the bride and bridegroom have indicated what they would like, and invariably the National Association of Flower Arrangers is commissioned to supply, design and arrange the tall cones that decorate the sacrarium where the marriages are conducted. Until the wedding of Princess Anne, these floral cones, often as high as nine feet, stood on either side of the high altar. In 1973 they were positioned at the top of the sacrarium steps where they were kept well back so as not to mask either the Royal Family or the Gentlemen-at-Arms.

Also in the Receiver-General's domain lies the hire of the exterior awning, the blue carpet which runs from the west gate to the foot of the sacrarium and the thousands of chairs to accommodate the guests, which are always turned to face the nave.

On the big day itself, the Receiver-General's duties are less onerous. Having satisfied himself that everybody inside the abbey knows what he is doing he can retire comfortably to the Chapel of St Edward the Confessor. There, because he is also Registrar, he will lay out the registers and, at the conclusion of the marriage ceremony, supervise their signature. Then, once the final fanfare has been sounded and the procession of the clergy has reached the organ screen, it falls to him to advise the royal bride and groom that it is time for them to be on their way. His last job of the day will be to take the abbey register to Buckingham Palace where, during the wedding-breakfast, he collects the signatures of members of the Royal Family who have not signed in the abbey. His duty fulfilled, he will return to the abbey, more often than not with the bride's bouquet which is placed on the Tomb of the

Westminster Abbey, London: the choir and sacrarium from the organ screen.

Unknown Warrior. As soon as possible after that, the great church is re-opened to the public.

One of the most complex jobs of all nowadays is the arrangements for radio and television broadcasts. Here, the unstinted co-operation of the Buckingham Palace press office is fully required. Under normal circumstances this office is worked to full capacity on the Royal Family's official schedule – quite apart from coping with enquiries from the press and public – so that an occasion like a royal wedding tends to intensify the pressure greatly. Nonetheless, the sovereign's press office manages to handle every aspect of the arrangements for the news media in a cool and efficient manner. The country's news agencies apply formally for the necessary press passes which are issued by the palace and used on a strict rota system. The majority of passes go to journalists since news reports, for variety if nothing else, need to be seen through the eyes of several different writers; the remaining passes are allocated to photographic agencies as photographs are, very often, shared among newspapers and journals.

Innumerable meetings of the departments I have mentioned take place during the preceding weeks and, so far as transmission of a royal wedding is concerned, representatives from the television companies are invited to take part – often at the Chapter Office of Westminster Abbey – in order that their requirements can be noted, their plans approved and positions for television cameras and special lighting, allocated. For Princess Anne's wedding, fifty cameras and three hundred engineers in fourteen mobile control rooms were utilized to transmit the service half-way round the world. Lighting was rigged up to flood the abbey with the unreal but necessary light of arc-lamps, together with specially positioned gold spotlights to make the most of the royal bride's immaculate complexion.

As a rule, there are three rehearsals of the wedding inside the abbey, and while they are designed basically to familiarize those taking part with their rôles, they are the only occasions on which the television companies can rehearse the parts they themselves must play on the day of the wedding. Monitor screens are erected in the body of the church for guests too distant to see what is happening, and there are also monitor screens for the broadcasters themselves. The entire programme is timed with a stop-watch and, as the expert broadcaster Audrey Russell pointed out to me, it is essential for a commentator to build his or her dialogue around a basic story. Any delays in royal arrivals for instance, can so easily result in a period of embarrassing silence while broadcaster and audience alike wonder what on earth has gone wrong. With a definite story line all but the gravest hold-ups can be professionally disguised.

But the ability to keep a commentary flowing is not the only requirement for a television broadcaster; a head for heights also helps, as Audrey Russell discovered for the first time in 1960 when she arrived at Westminster Abbey to cover Princess Margaret's wedding. 'Are you here to describe the hats?' one official asked. Miss Russell replied that she was there to describe the wedding. She was then shown

Crowds surround Buckingham Palace on Princess Mary's wedding day, 28 February 1922. The royal party is returning to the palace after the ceremony.

Lord John Hope, Minister of Works, inspects some gilded crowns, part of the lavish street decorations in 1960 for the wedding of Princess Margaret.

a narrow winding staircase which took her to the triphorium hundreds of feet above the nave itself; there she discovered the electricians and engineers and her 'seat' for the duration of the wedding ceremony – an unsecured builder's cradle. At one end sat a monitor screen and at the other end a cushion. Audrey Russell's misgivings about climbing into the 'flying coffin', as the box had been nicknamed, were understandable given the fact that there was nothing between the floor of the cradle and the nave. 'Then somebody produced a harness,' Miss Russell told me, 'which was like giving a trapeze artiste a safety net.' In the meantime, however, she had had time to compose herself and admitted that she slipped the harness off, 'just to prove to the others that I really was all right without it'.

Three years later, when she was asked to cover the wedding of Princess Alexandra from the same spot, Audrey Russell found some consolation in the fact that, this time, the cradle had not only been firmly secured to a nearby ledge, but the sides had also been boxed in.

It has taken many years for television companies and the press to win the confidence of the Royal Family. The joint venture between the BBC and ITV in making the 1969 film *Royal Family* was seen as a major break-through in this type of commercial coverage of the Royal Family's life, private and official, at home and abroad. Since then, the atmosphere between the Court and this aspect of the news media has become even more relaxed. When the Queen, as Princess Elizabeth, was married in Westminster Abbey in 1947, George VI made it quite clear that he did not wish photographers to be allowed further than the organ screen or, as it was put at the time, 'east of the nave'. Today, photographers' stands are erected – sometimes on two decks – above the great west door through which the Royal Family and their guests process; at certain sections along the nave; and indeed overlooking the sacrarium itself. In deference to the privacy of the Queen's family, the faces of the bridal couple are still not shown during the wedding ceremony. This mutual respect resulted in the BBC being invited into the balcony room of Buckingham Palace, following Princess Anne's wedding, to record scenes to be used as part of the Queen's 1973 Christmas Day broadcast to the United Kingdom and the Commonwealth.

In the Middle Ages, the public celebration of a royal wedding often lasted for as long as a week. Today, the celebration usually lasts for one day – the day of the wedding. But from that time several centuries ago, right up to the reign of Queen Victoria (as will be seen shortly), marriages within the Royal Family were strictly non-public events. Nowadays, while the arrangements for a royal wedding seem to be more complicated and certainly involve many more people, the public at large are able to participate in such a wedding to an unparalleled degree.

Scene of countless spectacular royal processions, the flag-bedecked Mall is arrayed to greet Princess Margaret on the return from the abbey.

2

The End of the Regency

Today nobody would expect a royal wedding to be celebrated at night ... but until Queen Victoria married Prince Albert of Saxe-Coburg in 1840, few royal marriages were ever solemnized at any other time of day. Such ceremonies, so far as the public were concerned, had their numerous drawbacks and any kind of participation on the part of loyal subjects was severely restricted. Queen Victoria's wedding, however, changed all that for she chose to break with tradition and set her own marriage service for one o'clock in the afternoon.

Nowadays, due to highly sophisticated technology, royal weddings have become the most public of private occasions. When Princess Anne married Captain Mark Phillips in 1973, for example, the wedding was witnessed by the largest 'congregation' in the history of television. Transmitted throughout Great Britain – the first time a royal wedding had been seen in colour – it was linked 'live' to the United States (where, because of the time difference dawn had hardly broken), throughout Europe to Japan.

Statisticians later estimated that Princess Anne's wedding had been viewed by some 530 million people, totalling 230 million more than had watched the wedding of Princess Margaret thirteen years before. Such figures illustrate the esteem in which the Queen and her family are held throughout the world. They must surely confound the sceptics and baffle, if not silence, the monarchy's inevitable critics, while leaving them to ponder the phenomenal response to occasions perhaps more suited to the days of the empire than those of the late twentieth century.

The prototype of the royal weddings we know today was that which founded the Victorian era and created a huge family extending across Europe and into Russia.

There is a legend which still survives that Queen Victoria and Prince Albert's marriage had been ordained from the time of their infancy (there was only three months difference in their ages; Victoria having been born in May 1819, and Albert in August of the same year). In reality, the Prince and Princess did not even meet until 1836; and even then Prince Albert hadn't arrived in England on a fine white charger all set to carry his cousin off to some Utopian paradise. It was no more than a family visit; two nephews, Albert and his brother Ernst, came to England to see their 'Aunt Kent' and cousin Victoria, at what was then officially called 'the King's Palace of Kensington'.

Princess Caroline of Brunswick in the dress she wore for her wedding. For some reason, the official painting showed her in different attire.

BELOW: The marriage of George, Prince of Wales, and Princess Caroline of Brunswick at the Chapel Royal, St James's Palace. King George III is seated behind the bride and Queen Charlotte behind the bridegroom.

It cannot be denied, however, that there were political as well as sentimental forces at work behind the trip; for the couple's common uncle Prince Leopold, later elected King of the Belgians, was the brother of both Victoria's mother and Albert's father and he was certainly very keen to encourage a marriage between his good-looking nephew and pretty young niece. It isn't difficult to understand why, when one remembers that Leopold had, once upon a time, stood in a similar position to Albert, having won the hand of the Prince Regent's only child, Princess Charlotte.

For Leopold it had been in every respect a highly advantageous marriage, especially since the Princess was next in line to the throne after her father, later King George IV. Had it not been for the inept bungling of the doctors when the time came for the Princess to give birth to her first child in 1817, Leopold himself would have become Prince Consort of England. As it was, after a gruelling period of labour lasting fifty-two hours, Princess Charlotte's baby – a son – was born dead. Three hours later, Princess Charlotte followed her baby to the grave.

From that moment the line of succession stood in jeopardy: there was no heir. George III's mind – because of the undiagnosed malady porphyria – grew rapidly more feeble and, although his eldest son George, Prince Regent since 1811, would succeed to the throne, he was already fifty-four and well past his prime. It was said that Prinny's high living had rendered him virtually impotent, but his virility was not the point in question. He and his wife, Caroline of Brunswick, lived apart – and since the very thought of physical contact was anathema to both parties there was no hope at all of them attempting to produce another child.

Where then to look for an heir? Logically Parliament turned its expectant gaze towards the Prince Regent's seven brothers. Four were already married but without children and of the three who were still single only Adolphus Frederick, Duke of Cambridge, could be looked upon as being clean-living. Unencumbered by mistresses or bastards he was certainly the most eligible of the princes.

William, Duke of Clarence, and Edward, Duke of Kent, on the other hand were already heavily committed. Prince William had a liaison with Dorothy Bland, a Dublin-born actress of questionable talent, better known as Mrs Jordan, who had provided him with ten illegitimate children (the FitzClarences) all of whom the Duke recognized as his own, and Prince Edward with Madame de St Laurent, a lady of obscure background with whom he had lived for twenty-seven years.

For all the princes, the unexpected demise of their niece, and Parliament's inevitable offer of renewed financial gain if they stirred themselves into action, meant that public interest was focused on their present relationships. Both Madame de St Laurent and Mrs Jordan were understandably mortified when their respective lovers finally decided to comply with the nation's pleas for help, though it was Adolphus Frederick who married first. In mid May 1818 he wedded the desirable Princess Augusta of Hesse-Cassel, a great-granddaughter of King George II. They were remarried a couple of weeks later, on 1 June, in the presence of Queen Charlotte in London.

In the interim, the Duke of Kent, with the aid of his close friend, Prince Leopold,

Princess Charlotte, the Prince Regent's only child, returning from her wedding at Carlton House during the evening of 2 May 1816. With her is her bridegroom, Prince Leopold of Saxe-Coburg-Saalfeld.

BELOW: The Dutch House at Kew, scene of the double wedding in 1818 of Prince William, Duke of Clarence, to Princess Adelaide of Saxe-Meiningen and Prince Edward, Duke of Kent, to Victoria Mary, Dowager Princess of Saxe-Meiningen.

the late Princess Charlotte's husband, arranged to marry Mary Victoria, Dowager Princess of Saxe-Meiningen, Leopold's sister.

At the same time, William of Clarence had chosen – somewhat reluctantly, given his feelings for Mrs Jordan – to marry Princess Adelaide of Saxe-Meiningen, a rather plain, evangelical young woman of twenty-six, who lived in perpetual fear of revolution. Both couples were married first in traditional evening ceremonies in their respective fiancées' homeland and then took part in a double wedding at Queen Charlotte's red-brick mansion, the Dutch House at Kew, during the late afternoon of 11 July 1818. This was the only time on record that a double wedding had been celebrated in British royal history, though in this instance it did at least mean that both couples had an equal chance in the race to provide the country with an heir.

Due to the frail condition of the dying Queen Charlotte, the joint wedding had to be postponed by two days, with the result that the guests arriving at Kew on Thursday 9 July were hurriedly advised to attend on Saturday the eleventh.

That day, the Prince Regent accompanied his mother as she entered the comparatively small ground-floor dining-room which was adorned with the magnificent gold plate brought especially from the Chapel Royal, St James's Palace, and laid like some bizarre sacrificial offering on top of the makeshift altar. The Dukes and Duchesses of York and Cambridge were present together with the Duchess of Gloucester, the bridegrooms' sister, the Landgrave of Hesse-Cassel and various members of the nobility.

The Bishop of London, Dean of the Chapel Royal, whose duty it was to enter the unions in the registers of the chapel, assisted the Archbishop of Canterbury in the celebration of the marriages.

The Dowager Princess Mary Victoria, wearing gold, and Princess Adelaide, in silver, entered the room, to be given away by the Prince Regent; the royal dukes joined their brides before the altar. As soon as the service (which took almost an hour) was over, a messenger took to his horse and rode to London with the news that England now had two new royal duchesses. The tidings were greeted with a double salute of gunfire and the sound of pealing bells all over the capital.

Queen Charlotte repaired to her room to pick at her meal alone while the wedding party celebrated at the picturesque cottage in the grounds of Kew which bore the Queen's name. In the large ground-floor salon of this quaint two-room structure, a huge banquet was set including a mountain of 'remarkably fine' fruit, all of which 'was served up in a very superior style and order'. Then the Clarences drove up to London to their apartments at St James's Palace, and the Kents, driving in Prince Leopold's 'chariot', left for Esher and Claremont, the mansion in which poor Princess Charlotte had died so recently. Little more than a month later, the Duke of Kent and his bride were bound for Amorbach. Mary Victoria may have become the first Duchess of Kent, but she was still Princess Regent of Saxe-Meiningen until such time as her fourteen-year-old son, Charles, had attained his majority and could rule in his own right.

By the time Queen Charlotte died in November, the Duchess of Kent was already

ABOVE: An engraving of Prince William, Duke of Clarence, made after he had become king.

ABOVE: Princess Adelaide of Saxe-Meiningen, the wife of William IV.

BELOW: Prince Edward, Duke of Kent, father of Queen Victoria.

BELOW: Victoria Mary, Duchess of Kent, at the time of her marriage in 1818.

expecting a baby. This child, born in London the following May, was to live up to a prophecy made by a gipsy to the Duke of Kent long before he married: 'You will have a daughter and she will become a great queen.'

What the gipsy did not foretell, however, was that the Duke would not live to see his daughter Victoria grow into girlhood, for his premature death in January 1820 followed her birth by only eight months. Nonetheless, there can be no greater epitaph to this man than that he provided the country with not only an heir but a princess to fill the void left by Princess Charlotte.

Twenty years later, history repeated itself when another prince of Saxe-Coburg set foot on British soil destined to become the husband of a future English queen. But this time it was the prince and not the princess who was to meet an untimely end.

It is difficult to judge the young Victoria's true reaction upon meeting Prince Albert for the first time because various conflicting reports still exist. Some say she was merely grateful to have the company of somebody her own age after a childhood that is best described as solitary. Other reports claim that the young princess was more than favourably impressed. Any clear decision is further hampered by the knowledge that Victoria's journals were known to have been scrutinized by her mother. In typically exaggerated fashion, Victoria described her cousin in an almost ceaseless flow of glowing adjectives. Among other things he was kind, honest, good, dear, gentle, beautiful and attentive. Ideal qualities for a future husband one would have thought. In any event, Victoria eventually made up her mind that she was both helplessly and hopelessly in love with Albert. As a result, two years after ascending the throne, she invited him to Windsor and there, in the summer of 1839, proposed to him. On 23 November that year, the Queen summoned her Privy Council to declare her intentions and Mr Charles Greville, then Clerk of the Council, recorded the scene as follows:

All the Privy Councillors seated themselves, when the folding-doors were thrown open, and the Queen came in, attired in a plain morning-gown, but wearing a bracelet containing Prince Albert's picture. She read the declaration in a clear, sonorous, sweet-toned voice, but her hands trembled so excessively that I wonder she was able to read the paper she held. Lord Lansdowne made a little speech, asking her permission to have the declaration made public. She bowed assent, placed the paper in his hands, and then retired.

Three days later Greville noted:

The Queen wrote to all her family and announced her marriage to them. When she saw the Duchess of Gloucester in town, and told her she was to make her declaration the next day, the Duchess asked her if it was a nervous thing to do. She said, 'Yes; but I did a much more nervous thing a little while ago.' 'What was that?' 'I proposed to Prince Albert.'

Queen Victoria was in the unusual position, so far as the Royal Family are concerned, of not having to ask anybody's consent to her marriage. Indeed, her plans were already well in hand before Lord Melbourne, both her prime minister and hitherto

ABOVE: Queen Victoria's bridal
veil and wreath of orange blossom.

Queen Victoria dressed in white satin and Honiton lace for her wedding to Prince Albert of
Saxe-Coburg-Gotha on 10 February 1840.

her mentor, had any firm notion of what was afoot. Not that he presumed to enquire what the Queen's intentions were, noted Mr Greville, but:

> It was his duty to tell her that if she had any [plans for marriage] it was necessary that her ministers should be apprised of them. She said she had nothing to tell him, and about a fortnight afterwards she informed him that the whole thing was settled. A curious exhibition of her independence. . . .

Hypothetically, had Victoria still been a princess at that time, regardless of whether she was next in line to the throne or not, she would have been obliged under the terms of the Royal Marriages Act of 1772 to seek the sovereign's consent.

The Act, regulating the marriages of members of the royal house, had been introduced by Victoria's grandfather, King George III, from necessity and a deep-seated conviction that, as monarch, it fell to him to raise the moral standard of the English court and rid his kingdom of 'vice, profaneness and immorality'.

George III had good reason to be concerned about the image of the House of Hanover. The first two Georges had hardly been paragons of virtue and, within his own family, his three brothers, Edward, William, and Henry, the Dukes of York, Gloucester and Cumberland, had found themselves in situations that were potentially harmful to the royal line. Had they not had such insatiable sexual appetites, the King would never have had cause for concern.

The death of Edward, Duke of York, in 1767 removed one obstacle from the King's precarious path, but Gloucester and Cumberland persisted with their amorous pursuits.

Cumberland was responsible for a scandal which not only resulted in the end of a marriage but found the unfortunate monarch – not his guilty brother – paying out some £13,000 compensation to the injured husband. But that was incidental to the Duke's obvious love of 'wenching', and a little later a tale was spread that he had married a young woman by the name of Olive Wilmot, a clergyman's daughter. Insult was added to injury when, within the same space of twelve months, Cumberland met, fell in love with and married a widow by the name of Anne Horton! The truth of the matter remains a mystery, but one thing is abundantly clear: George III would certainly not have given his consent to either marriage and if indeed the marriage to Mistress Wilmot did take place then the Duke was guilty of bigamy.

In the meantime, William of Gloucester had been carefully concealing his own marriage from the King. At the age of twenty-three, he had taken a bride some fourteen years his senior, the Dowager Countess Waldegrave, illegitimate daughter of Sir Robert Walpole's son Edward.

The last straw, however, was the realization that the King's sister, Caroline Matilda, the wife of Christian VII, the 'mad' boy-king of Denmark, was having an illicit affair with one of her husband's advisers. When the truth was revealed the Queen was banished from the kingdom and her lover was put to death.

Small wonder therefore that George III saw fit to curb the excesses of so free a

An engraving of the young Queen and her consort after the wedding, showing her wearing the riband of the Order of the Garter. While she certainly wore the ornate collar of the Order this was one of the few important occasions when the riband was not worn.

family as his own. Hence the introduction of the Royal Marriages Act which, while being unable to prevent the extramarital activities of his brothers and sisters, would, at least, safeguard the future line of succession. In the act, the King proclaimed that no descendant of George II would be permitted to marry *without* the sovereign's consent; and if such consent were to be withheld, the prince or princess in question could give one year's formal notice to the Privy Council of his or her intentions. Then, if neither of the Houses of Parliament contested the issue, the marriage could go ahead and would be considered valid.

As Queen, however, Victoria was able to dispense with this formality completely and on Monday 10 February 1840, three months after the formal announcement of her betrothal, she rode in state to the Chapel Royal, St James's Palace, for her wedding to Albert of Saxe-Coburg.

The weather was appalling, 'torrents of rain, and violent gusts of wind', recorded Greville; but for all that the town was swarming with Londoners determined to enjoy the event. They thronged St James's Park and although long-distance transport into London had yet to be perfected, Greville noted that he had 'never beheld such a congregation'.

For Queen Victoria, however, only one person mattered, her 'dear, good' Albert. She wrote to him that morning:

Dearest,

How are you today, and have you slept well? I have rested very well and feel very comfortable today. What weather! I believe, however, the rain will cease.

Send one word when you, my most dearly beloved bridegroom, will be ready.

Thy ever faithful,
Victoria R.

Upon her arrival at St James's Palace, the young Queen, 'perfectly composed and quiet', processed through the state rooms *en route* to the Chapel Royal, attended by her twelve bridesmaids. One of them, Lady Wilhelmina Stanhope, later Duchess of Cleveland, complained that the Queen's train, although eighteen feet long, was 'rather too short for the number of young ladies who carried it'. Stressing what she meant, Lady Wilhelmina went on to describe how the bridesmaids 'were all huddled together, and scrambled rather than walked along, kicking each other's heels and treading on each other's gowns'.

Ten minutes before the Queen's arrival, a trumpet fanfare had welcomed Prince Albert to the chapel and, dressed in the scarlet and white uniform of a British field-marshal with his bridal favours at his shoulder and the Star and riband of the Most Noble Order of the Garter proudly worn across his chest, the bridegroom made an impressive picture. He advanced to the altar to the curiously chosen strains of Handel's *See the Conquering Hero Comes*, and seemed, so contemporary reports tell us, so pensive as to have been completely oblivious to the blatant adulation of all the young ladies present, to whom he did indeed appear something of a hero.

Then, to the sounds of a renewed flourish and the boom of the chapel's organ, the Queen herself arrived; her hand resting lightly on the arm of her uncle, the Duke of Sussex, who was to give her away. Her lovely gown of white satin, with its low neckline, was adorned with a deep flounce of white Honiton lace worked to an antique design, the chain of the Garter hung round her shoulders, and a coronet of orange blossom discreetly studded with a handful of diamonds secured a short veil of lace.

When Albert made his vows, the Queen's eyes filled with tears, noted one observer and one continental journalist (they were apparently admitted even in those days) commented that, 'this was her hour of beauty'.

Indeed, as at her coronation, Victoria combined both the dignity of a sovereign and the sheer wonderment of a twenty-year-old who has just discovered the joy of overwhelming affection. It was a curious position; for here was a young Queen who had never known the love of a father, and a young prince with nothing but distant memories of the mother he adored who had died so young in exile. It isn't difficult to imagine what Victoria and Albert represented to each other.

After the wedding service, Victoria, whose face was rather more flushed than when she arrived, fondly kissed her aunt, the Dowager Queen Adelaide, shook hands with her mother – an action which gave rise to some sharp-tongued comment afterwards – and was led back to the crimson and gold throne room by her new husband to sign the marriage registers. Then after the Queen had presented a gift brooch (an eagle, after Albert's crest, set with turquoise and pearls) to each of her bridesmaids, the party adjourned to Buckingham Palace for a celebratory banquet during which the newly married couple cut their wedding-cake. This was, in itself, something of a masterpiece. Weighing three hundred pounds, it had a circumference of nine feet, was adorned by a figure of Britannia with cupids at her feet (one of whom held a book on which was written the date of the wedding), and had cost a hundred guineas to make.

Then, shortly after four o'clock in the afternoon, it was time for the bride and bridegroom to leave London for Windsor and a four-day honeymoon. Over and above this joyous respite, duty called and when Prince Albert remonstrated that a mere two or three days was hardly sufficient for a honeymoon, Victoria bristled: 'You forget, my dearest love, that I am the sovereign and that business can stop and wait for nothing. Parliament is sitting and something occurs almost every day for which I am required ...'

Victoria's imperious tantrums were, however, short-lived where Albert was concerned, and during the evening of her wedding-day, she took a moment away from her bridegroom to record in her journal the scene of their arrival in Windsor:

Our reception was most enthusiastic and gratifying in every way; the people quite deafening us; and horsemen and gigs etc. driving along with us. We came through Eton where all the boys received us most kindly – and cheered and shouted. Really I was quite touched ... We only arrived at 7.

Before we move on, let us at this point consider bridal fashion, particularly since

Queen Victoria was responsible for choosing an outfit unlike any of those worn by her predecessors.

Until the end of the eighteenth century it was considered fashionable for the robes of the bridegroom to vie in splendour with those of his bride. Trains, silk stockings, velvet overmantles, satin shoes adorned with rosettes and cloth of silver were frequently found among the groom's wedding-day apparel until this trend slowly became more sober and military uniform like that worn by Prince Albert was adopted.

The bride has always been expected to steal the show, and until the advent of Queen Victoria's wedding, royal females often went to their weddings in an array of over-decorated fabrics and costly, ostentatious hair ornaments. The wedding-dress of the Danish princess, Sophia Magdalena, who married King Gustavus III of Sweden in 1766, was a prime example, presenting a spectacle that was the source of endless comment. Her dress was cut to accommodate wide hoops of silver and white brocade patterned with roses within diamonds, the fabric trailing away to form a long train. The design of this gown – still preserved in Stockholm – was believed to have been of French origin; it was very similar to the gown worn five years earlier by Princess Charlotte of Mecklenburg-Strelitz, Queen Victoria's grandmother, for her wedding to King George III in 1761. On this occasion the silver brocade was woven with patterns of flowers – some say carnations – in three types of gold thread. To complement the gown, Charlotte wore a purple velvet cap covered with diamonds and from her shoulders fell an 'endless train' of purple velvet edged with ermine.

In 1795 Queen Charlotte's despised daughter-in-law, Caroline of Brunswick, wore a net dress heavily embroidered once again in silver with an underdress and train of shimmering silver tissue. With it Caroline chose to wear her royal mantle of crimson velvet trimmed with ermine and on her head a small bejewelled crown – something of a change from ostrich feathers affixed to diamond bandeaux, the prevailing fashion. Her hair, according to an ancient custom, was worn loose over her shoulders as a symbol of virginity. In Princess Caroline's case, however, virginity was a highly questionable state. Her easy manner had given rise to a command from her father that she was not to be left alone with a man and, even when she danced, had to be shadowed by her governess in an attempt to prevent the Princess from engaging her partner in risqué conversation.

In 1816, Caroline's daughter, the ill-fated Princess Charlotte, was married during the evening of 2 May in the Great Crimson Room of her father's home, Carlton House. On this occasion the bride wore a high-waisted gown of white silk net embroidered in silver strips on a spotted background, bordered with flowers, leaves and shells. Once again, the almost obligatory silver underskirt was worn and a long silver tissue train was edged with a deep net frill. The bride's head-dress on this occasion, however, was a simple affair, a wreath of roses set round her hair which was worn 'up'.

Compared to her predecessors Queen Victoria's wedding-gown was charmingly simple. But the popular use of silver had not yet had its day, as will be seen further on. In the interim, however, ostentation of a different kind found its way into the design of some of the later Victorian wedding-dresses. Many of these gowns were so heavily festooned and garlanded with leaves and orange blossom that the wearers tended to resemble a variety of exotic horticultural exhibits rather than wide-eyed brides.

3

Cousinhood across Europe

Queen Victoria and Prince Albert were married for twenty-one years and during that time the Queen gave birth to no fewer than nine children: Victoria (the Princess Royal), Albert Edward (later Edward VII), Alice, Alfred, Helena (known as Lenchen), Louise, Arthur, Leopold and Beatrice (sometimes known as 'Baby'). Yet when the time came for these princes and princesses to marry there seemed to be something of a reversal of the old order; for, with the exception of the marriage of the Princess Royal to Prince Frederick William of Prussia in 1858, the remaining children of the family were married in private ceremonies, held either at Windsor or on the Isle of Wight.

The idea of private weddings did not, understandably, suit the bulk of the population at all. They might not be able to travel far themselves but they did want to know what was going on! Victoria would have none of it. She reasoned that since the Court had been in (continual) mourning for Prince Albert, who died of typhoid in December 1861 at the untimely age of forty-two, she had no wish to be gawped at by the public in what she over-dramatically termed, her 'grief'.

The first of Victoria's children to marry under the prevailing cloud of mourning was Princess Alice, the Queen's third child and second daughter. Alice had become engaged in 1861 to Prince Louis, later Grand Duke of Hesse. Applauded as the 'angel in the house' during her father's fatal illness and in the weeks following his death, Alice's first reaction was to forsake her own happiness and cancel her marriage. By so doing she could thus remain at home with her inconsolable mother. Deeply moved though she was by her daughter's devotion, but equally determined to carry through every one of 'his' (Albert's) wishes, Queen Victoria insisted that Alice and Louis should be married as planned. Victoria's altruism did not, however, extend to the type of wedding 'he' would surely have wished for the daughter to whom he had become particularly attached following the Princess Royal's marriage. And so on 1 July 1862 – an overcast, blustery day – Alice's wedding passed off under the most subdued and sombre of conditions.

The dining-room at Osborne overlooking Prince Albert's Italian garden was turned into a temporary chapel, a makeshift altar was erected under a painting of the family in happier times, at which the Queen gazed with tears rolling down her cheeks; the Archbishop of Canterbury, in the same emotional state, performed the ceremony; and the ladies of the household-in-waiting were given permission to exchange their mourning dresses for outfits of grey or violet. Victoria herself stuck rigidly to her widow's weeds, relieved only by the familiar white tulle cap.

Princess Alice entered the 'chapel' wearing a crinoline of white lace, together with the veil her father had designed for her. There followed a cheerless lunch with her mother and bridegroom in the small ground-floor Horn Room, surrounded by furnishings made from the antlers of deer hunted by the Prince Consort. Immediately afterwards, the endless mourning garments reappeared – even the bride herself being obliged to revert to the black dresses she had worn for the past year.

Yet if most of Victoria's subjects were prepared to overlook one royal wedding being held behind closed doors, they were not so compassionate eight months later when Bertie, the Prince of Wales, married Princess Alexandra of Denmark at St George's Chapel, Windsor Castle. On that occasion one popular journal contended that if the Queen wished the marriage of her son and heir to pass off unnoticed, then a simple announcement in *The Times* along the lines: 'On 10 March 1863 at St George's Chapel, Windsor, Edward England to Alexandra Denmark' would have been sufficient press coverage.

Queen Victoria remained unmoved. Bertie's would *not* be a public marriage! In July 1885 there was, however, some small change of heart over the wedding of Princess Beatrice and Prince Henry of Battenberg. At first Victoria would not even hear of 'Baby' getting married, but having secured from the couple a promise that they would continue to live with her, the Queen relented and gave her consent.

Once again there could be an element of public participation, for the wedding was to be celebrated not in London nor at Windsor but in the small parish church of St Mildred, Whippingham, which stood near Osborne on the Isle of Wight. And after all her initial reticence the Queen turned out to be delighted by what she termed her daughter's 'village wedding'. It is also interesting to note that on this occasion the Queen gave the bride away herself.

Both the nineteenth century and the record-breaking reign of Queen Victoria began moving to a close with the most significant royal marriage for thirty years. In 1893 the future King George V, Victoria's sailor grandson and 'founder' of the royal house of Windsor, married Princess May of Teck. There was in fact something about this particular betrothal that puts one in mind of the first marriage of Henry VIII. For on 11 June 1509 the second son of Henry VII and Elizabeth of York was married to Katherine, daughter of King Ferdinand V of Aragon and II of Sicily, the 24-year-old widow of his elder brother, Arthur. Nearly four hundred years later Prince George, Duke of York, himself a second son, was about to marry the princess who had first been betrothed to his elder brother, Albert Victor, Duke of Clarence.

Princess May, the tall, rather wistful-looking daughter of Francis, Duke of Teck, and his rotund wife, Princess Mary of Cambridge – a cousin of Queen Victoria – became engaged to Prince Albert Victor, Duke of Clarence, 'Eddy' to his family,

The Weddings of the

Children of Queen Victoria

ABOVE: Queen Victoria's second daughter, Princess Alice, on her wedding-day.

LEFT: Queen Victoria's children were married in a variety of settings as these contemporary illustrations show.
Centre the Princess Royal married Prince Frederick William of Prussia in the Chapel Royal, St James's Palace, on 25 January 1858.
Top left the marriage of the Duke of Connaught with Princess Louis-Margaret of Prussia in St George's Chapel, Windsor, on 13 March 1879.
Top right the wedding of Princess Louise and the Marquess of Lorne at St George's Chapel, Windsor, on 21 March 1871.
Below left Princess Alice's wedding to Prince Louis of Hesse at Osborne on 1 July 1862.
Below right Prince Alfred, Duke of Edinburgh, married Grand Duchess Marie of Russia in the Winter Palace, St Petersburg, on 23 January 1874.

at the beginning of 1892. Some said that he didn't much care for May but it was he who proposed and although it would in effect have been an arranged marriage, he did so a month earlier than had been originally planned. All the same there did seem something a little odd about this elder son of the Prince and Princess of Wales. In his lessons he was apathetic and backward. At home his gentleness and overt good nature irritated his father as much as it endeared him to his mother, but even she, when Eddy reached the age of nineteen and showed no real signs of progress, began to despair. After all, this was the man who, at that time, stood to inherit the throne of England.

Eddy, however, seemed less interested in his heritage than having a good time and this, not surprisingly, gave rise to gossip in the outer world and concern within his family. As with his lessons, he found it impossible to concentrate on one love affair at a time and he fell in and out of love at an alarming rate – often with the most unsuitable types. As James Pope-Hennessy put it in his biography of Queen Mary, 'among the few things Prince Eddy really cared for was every form of dissipation and amusement'. Indeed, the twentieth century was to reveal rather more about this prince than could have been stomached during the reign of his grandmother. There was, for instance, talk of an illegitimate child born to a street-girl in what is now St Stephen's Hospital, Fulham; homosexual liaisons and an ominous link with the Whitechapel murderer who, at various intervals during 1888, mutilated five prostitutes. It would be impossible to identify the Prince himself as Jack the Ripper, but a cloud of mystery shrouds Eddy's rumoured involvement to this day. This is made more tantalizing by the fact that the private papers of both his parents were – at their command – destroyed upon their respective deaths.

After a brief, but doomed engagement to Hélène, the Comte de Paris' daughter (doomed because the Princess was forbidden to forsake her Roman Catholic religion) Eddy had become engaged to Princess Victoria Mary of Teck, known widely as May. As with his father before him, marriage was considered the only remedy for Eddy's giddy way of life. It seems strange that marriage should be seen as the finest cure for the wayward male; although in the case of Edward VII, it did little to cool his passion, as a string of mistresses, including Lillie Langtry, Daisy Warwick, 'Skittles' (Catherine Walters) and Alice Keppel, bears testimony.

The marriage between Prince Albert Victor and Princess May, arranged for 27 February 1892, was not to be. Little more than six weeks before the wedding-day Eddy suddenly died. Just after his twenty-eighth birthday, influenza led to inflammation of the lungs, and hours of agony finally gave way to peace. During delirium Eddy suddenly asked, 'Who is that?' and was gone.

It might be that had Eddy survived and married May of Teck the responsibility of a wife and, no doubt, a family, would have had its desired calming effect. It seems unlikely however, and in all probability the new Duchess of Clarence would have been led a merry dance. Instead, after a suitably decorous period, May became betrothed to Eddy's younger brother George who now occupied the position of heir apparent, once removed. Everybody agreed that the match was a wise move and

Queen Victoria's youngest child, Princess Beatrice, on her wedding-day, 23 July 1885.

The Times echoed the popular sentiment that, 'a union rooted in painful memories may prove happy beyond the common lot'.

The summer of 1893 typified the kind of hot, sultry weather that one associates with summers of long ago; but for the crowds waiting beneath the blue skies of London on the royal wedding-day, 6 July, the heat must have been as overwhelming as the colourful pageantry they were there to witness. A lively impression of the scene was given by the gossip columnist of *The Sketch* who, having told his readers that he had taken a hot bath (as some recompense for not managing to break through the dense crowds to join some friends along the processional route), noted:

I mixed on wedding-day with the unwashed in St James's Park. Heavens! how unsavoury is hot humanity. The sun poured down, the people steamed up, while smiles and good humour reigned over all. I clung to the railings before the palace, kept a handkerchief offering incense to my nose, and for reward saw everything. But the crowd, how patiently it waited and how readily it laughed! I will swear to the fact that several obese old ladies within my range offered gratuities to strange males for a friendly hoist when the carriages were coming, so dreadfully intent were they on a view. 'Blowed if I ain't more dead beat after that than a day's Parcels Post,' said a jolly postman, depositing his fair burden on mother earth, and pocketing the agreed fee of eighteen pence. 'You didn't 'old me 'igh enough,' cried another dissatisfied dame, 'and I'll only give you sixpence.' Extreme merriment was caused when a seedy man, under the influence of ginger beer and sun probably, sat down in the middle of the cleared roadway, and declined to move until four policemen united their persuasions. For comicality and stolid good nature commend me to an English mob.

The anonymous columnist's English mob remained in fine form all day and, as Queen Victoria passed by, dressed in black satin draped with white lace, her own wedding veil worn down her back, held by a small crown of diamonds, the streets were filled with a mighty roar which, predictably, rose again at the sight of the bridegroom, his cousin, the Tsarevich Nicholas of Russia – in looks they might almost have been identical twins – and, of course, the bride herself.

As she entered the Chapel Royal of St James's Palace, the old Queen leaned heavily on her stick while moving towards her chair attended by the bride's mother, and the Grand Duke of Hesse. Prince George of York then arrived with his father and his uncle, the Duke of Edinburgh, all dressed in naval uniform – the bridegroom in that of a captain and his father and uncle as Admirals of the Fleet.

Finally came the bride, dressed in white satin brocade embroidered with silver roses, thistles and shamrocks, festooned with orange blossom. The skirt, open at the front, revealed a satin underskirt and her full train was carried by her small attendants: Alice of Battenberg, Margaret and Patricia of Connaught, Beatrice of Edinburgh and Victoria of Battenberg. Then followed her five adult bridesmaids – and a plainer lot could never have been imagined. With the exception of the bridegroom's two sisters, Princesses Victoria and Maud of Wales, the three remaining attendants were all cousins of the bridegroom, Princess Alexandra of Edinburgh, Princess Victoria of Schleswig-Holstein and Princess Victoria of Edinburgh.

ABOVE: Prince George, Duke of York, is married to Princess May of Teck in the Chapel Royal, St James's, on 6 July 1893.

BELOW: The Duke and Duchess of York and their attendants. From left to right, back row: Princess Alexandra of Edinburgh, Princess Helena Victoria of Schleswig-Holstein, Princess Victoria Melita of Edinburgh, Princess Victoria and Princess Maud of Wales. Seated: Princess Alice of Battenberg, Princess Margaret of Connaught, Princess Beatrice of Edinburgh, Princess Victoria Eugenie of Battenberg and Princess Patricia of Connaught.

The silver and white procession passed under Holbein's ribbed ceiling to the bridal march from *Lohengrin* and then, with their families grouped around them, the couple were married by the Archbishop of Canterbury assisted by an assortment of other bishops and deans. After the vows had been exchanged and the couple proclaimed man and wife, the Duke and Duchess of York turned and kissed the hands of an appreciative Queen Victoria before returning to Buckingham Palace and a wedding-breakfast held in the throne room.

Later that day, the Duke and his bride drove through a bedecked London town to Liverpool Street Station to board a train for a less spectacular honeymoon in the cramped surroundings of York Cottage at Sandringham. It must also have been, for both George and May, an eerie start to what transpired to be one of the most successful and firm royal partnerships: they honeymooned in the same little house where Albert Victor had died only eighteen months before.

When the new century came in, however, changes in style were inevitable and not only would royal couples be looking further afield for idyllic places to honeymoon but they would also veer further away from the smaller weddings the Royal Family had known for so long under Queen Victoria, no matter how grand the proceedings themselves.

In this respect, Westminster Abbey, long the setting for coronations, came into its own as the church in which most members of the twentieth-century Royal Family chose to be married. It is the place that most people tend to associate with a royal wedding today. But until one of Princess May of Teck's own bridesmaids chose to be married at Westminster no royal weddings had been solemnized in the abbey since the thirteenth century. The earliest wedding on record was that of Henry I to Eadygyth – more commonly known as Matilda – the daughter of Malcolm Canmore, King of Scotland, which took place there on 11 November 1100. This was followed in 1269 by the marriage of Prince Edmund 'Crouchback', Earl of Lancaster, and Aveline, the daughter of the Count of Albemarle. Six centuries were to separate that royal wedding from the next, but once the abbey had become established as the setting for such ceremonies its registers were to chronicle, in quite a unique way, the lives of Britain's royal dynasty.

4

Between the Wars

The current trend for royal marriages to be celebrated at Westminster Abbey was set, albeit unwittingly, by Queen Victoria's granddaughter, Princess Patricia of Connaught, when she married Commander the Hon. Alexander Ramsay on Thursday 27 February 1919.

Following her marriage, this hugely popular Princess became something of a forgotten royal figure for reasons that will become clear shortly. But during her twenties and early thirties she was widely respected not only for what we today would call her 'common touch' but because of her highly developed individuality.

In fact, one American contemporary was moved to write: 'Of all the women I have known, Princess Patricia seems to me the most perfect. She is beautiful and good ... such a fine cultured young woman. ... I have never known anyone like her.'

Her Royal Highness Princess Victoria Patricia Helena Elizabeth of Connaught had been born at Buckingham Palace on St Patrick's Day, 17 March 1886, the second and youngest daughter of Queen Victoria's favourite son Arthur, Duke of Connaught.

Given the times in which they lived, Princess Patricia and her elder sister, Margaret (later Crown Princess of Sweden). were rather more progressively brought-up than most of their royal contemporaries. Indeed, it was said that the Princess – very much a part of a male-dominated society – held views on the suffragette movement that shocked some of her elder female relatives. Patsy, as she was known to her family, was a very artistic woman and she had her own studio at Clarence House (her father's London home). Later in life, some of her works were given public exhibitions. Not every member of the Royal Family understood her talents in that direction, and in her memoirs Princess Marie-Louise recalled that her cousin's paintings were 'rather modern – in fact, very modern', but she did concede that they were 'brilliantly clever'.

Despite the Princess's great popularity, however, when her engagement was announced towards the end of 1918 a grand-scale royal wedding was not planned. Nonetheless, her wedding had the same tonic-like effect on the nation that attended the marriage of Princess Elizabeth twenty-eight years later. After four gruelling years of war, the British were certainly in the mood for a celebration.

Princess Patricia was thirty-two when, having already declined offers of marriage from both King Alfonso of Spain and Grand Duke Cyril of Russia, she finally married the younger son of the thirteenth Earl of Dalhousie. Commander the Hon. Alexander Ramsay, a tall, dark-haired man, had been the Duke of Connaught's ADC when he became Governor-General of Canada in 1911. It was in Canada that the couple first met. As the health of the Duchess of Connaught (formerly Princess Louise-Margaret of Prussia) failed, her daughter was required to step in and assist the Duke in his official duties. When the Duchess died, it fell to Princess Pat, as she had been nicknamed by the Canadians, to fill the void as far as she was able as her father's companion and official government hostess. All this she accomplished with a verve and panache which endeared her to everybody with whom she came into contact, and resulted in the kind of press any public figure must dream of. (On the subject of her wedding alone, her father was able to compile two volumes of cuttings, now housed at Windsor.)

The Princess's reputation was enhanced even further in 1914 by her unstinted efforts in raising the regiment that was to bear her name – Princess Patricia's Light Infantry. As a special note of interest, the banner she personally worked and presented to the regiment was believed to have been the only colour carried by British troops throughout the battles on the Western Front during the Great War.

Princess Patricia's wedding, although in retrospect more 'high society' than royal (at least in the accepted sense) was, as King George V noted, 'a most popular marriage'. The crowds, whose enthusiasm according to *The Times* was 'almost embarrassing' despite England's dank February weather, were out in force, with only the London policemen in ceremonial uniform to hold them in line. The Royal Family were out in force too, Court mourning for young Prince John, son of the King and Queen who had died the previous month, having been waived for the occasion. And it was an impressive list of Victorian, Edwardian and 'modern-Georgian' royalty who assembled in the nave of the abbey. King George V was there with Queen Mary and Queen Alexandra; Queen Amelie, King Manoel and Queen Augusta Victoria came from Portugal; the Prince of Wales arrived back from a visit to France the day before; Edward VII's daughters, the Princess Royal and the Princess Victoria, were there, and so too were three of Queen Victoria's daughters: Princess Louise, Duchess of Argyll, Princess Helena (known as Princess Christian), and Princess Beatrice. The Duchess of Albany, Prince and Princess Arthur of Connaught, Princess Alice, Countess of Athlone and the Earl of Athlone (Queen Mary's brother), Princess Marie-Louise and Princess Helena-Victoria completed the royal party.

The invitations extended by the bride's father stated that morning dress should be worn and added that serving officers should wear service dress with swords. So far as a guard of honour was concerned, *The Times* announced that a detachment of Princess Patricia's Light Infantry would be mounted at the abbey's west door and a lining party of seamen from the bridegroom's ship, *King George V*, would be positioned along the nave.

A special note of interest concerning this wedding was the bride's decision to drop

Princess Patricia of Connaught in 1908. The
photograph is signed 'Patsy', the name by which she
was known to her family.

the title 'Princess' together with her standing as a Royal Highness; hence her gradual disappearance from the public memory which, at the best of times, is short.

The formal announcement of the Princess's decision, made public shortly before the wedding read:

In accordance with the express wish of HRH Princess Patricia of Connaught and with the concurrence of HRH the Duke of Connaught, the King has approved that subsequent to Her Royal Highness's marriage she relinquishes the above title, styling and rank, and assumes the name of Lady Patricia Ramsay.

It was a decision applauded not only by the press, who said, 'with her wedding she has put aside the Princess – an act in the true tradition of British aristocracy, that has always scorned the mere empty parade of titles for titles' sake'; but also by the Most Rev. Randall Davidson, Archbishop of Canterbury, who saw the Princess's act as 'a sign of the new spirit of national union which the war and its perils ... have created among the people'.

Yet despite the general euphoria it was almost unheard of for a British princess to renounce her titles, and any precedent that may already have been set lay too far in the past to be recalled. It should be said, however, that the Constitution does not officially require a Princess to relinquish her titles and rank on marriage and in Princess Patricia's case the decision to do so was her own; no doubt designed to bring herself closer in rank to that of her husband.

In any event, technical points aside, this picturesque wedding got under way on the morning of 27 February as the bride drove from Clarence House in one of the King's everyday road landaus with its hood pulled up. The carriage – the equivalent of one of the Queen's official Rolls-Royce state cars today – was drawn by four grey horses ridden by postillions in blue jackets and white breeches (known as 'scarlet liveries' when, as on this occasion, a royal carriage is attended by scarlet-clad outriders).

At the west door of Westminster Abbey – the usual entrance for royalty on such occasions incidentally – a striped awning had been erected as far as the west gate and a red carpet rolled out over the cobble-stoned forecourt. As the bride arrived she pulled her white ermine cloak around her shoulders, scooped up her skirt and train, and made her entry to a flourish of trumpets. Inside the abbey waited her eight bridesmaids and two page-boys. The adult maids, all in ankle-length dresses of pale blue taffeta and wide-brimmed picture hats, were: Princess Mary (daughter of King George and Queen Mary), Princess Maud of Fife (younger daughter of Louise, Princess Royal and sister of Princess Arthur of Connaught), and the Ladies Victoria and Helena Cambridge. The younger attendants were the bride's niece, Princess Ingrid of Sweden, Lady May Cambridge (daughter of Princess Alice and Lord Athlone), Lady Ira Ramsay (a niece of the bridegroom), Lady Jean Ramsay, the Hon. Simon Ramsay (a small tousled-haired boy who bore a marked resemblance to the subject of the famous 'Bubbles' painting) and the Earl of Macduff (son of Prince and Princess Arthur of Connaught).

ABOVE: Princess Patricia and her husband, Commander the Hon. Alexander Ramsay, after their wedding at Westminster Abbey on 27 February 1919.

DAILY SKETCH, FRIDAY, FEBRUARY 28, 1919.

HOW LONDON CHEERED THE BRIDAL PAIR : PAGES OF PICTURES.

DAILY SKETCH.

Telephones { London—Holborn 8312. Manchester—City 6361.   LONDON, FRIDAY, FEBRUARY 28, 1919.   [Registered as a Newspaper.]   ONE PENNY.

PRINCESS PATRICIA A SAILOR'S BRIDE.

The *Daily Sketch* the day after the wedding.

When she had removed her cloak, Princess Patricia stood for a moment or two with her father whilst her train was arranged. Her Venetian-style wedding-gown was a lovely creation of white broché panne and silver lace with a cloth-of-silver train embroidered with a design of lilies. Acorns and true lovers' knots trimmed the outfit and her antique rectangular lace veil – once owned by Queen Charlotte – picked up the theme of acorns and oak leaves. A narrow band of myrtle and leaves worn over her forehead held the veil in place, and instead of carrying a bouquet of multi-coloured anemones like her attendants, the bride chose to pin a small corsage of white heather and myrtle to her bodice.

Princess Patricia and Commander Ramsay were married by the Archbishop of Canterbury, assisted by Dean Ryle, and in his address to the couple, the Archbishop said:

If we look afield into the world's life we find the whole round earth athrob at a great juncture between war and peace ... to be married at such an hour, in such a place, is a wonderful, a priceless thing. It links your new start with the whole world's new endeavour; and the *genius loci*, the illustrious memories which belong to the most historic church in Christendom must uplift and invigorate and inspire.

At the end of the ceremony, the new Lady Patricia Ramsay and her husband drove back to Clarence House in their road landau, this time with the hood thrown back, while the rest of the Royal Family took to their cars and sped back to St James's Palace by another route to await their arrival.

The wedding luncheon, for about fifty guests, and hosted by the bride's father, the Duke of Connaught, was held in the palace's picture gallery. In mid-afternoon, the bride and bridegroom – both keen golfers – drove out of the palace gates in an open-topped car *en route* to Sutton Place and a golfing honeymoon.

When they returned to London, the former princess and her husband lived for a time at Clarence House – Lady Patricia having now, in all respects, become a private citizen – before moving to Ribsden Holt in Bagshot which was to remain their home for the rest of their lives.

By the time the 1920s turned the corner few of the world's thrones remained confidently on *terra firma*, and within the next twenty years many had completely vanished. Already the Russians had rid themselves of the Romanovs and Germany had bidden farewell to her egocentric Kaiser. The glut of marriageable princes had begun its decline. By 1922 when Princess Mary, the only daughter of King George V, was married, Britain's royal alliances with foreign royal houses had almost come to a halt. Apart from the recruitment of Princess Marina and Prince Philip of Greece there were to be no further marriages with members of foreign royal families.

Instead the scene was now set for the entry of so-called commoners; and in 1921 Princess Mary's engagement to Henry, Viscount Lascelles, which had received the King's blessing during the Royal Family's stay at York Cottage, Sandringham, was announced.

Viscount Lascelles and his
best man, Sir Victor
Mackenzie, arrive at
Westminster Abbey for the
royal wedding.

BELOW: Princess Mary
driving to her wedding at
Westminster Abbey in the
Irish State Coach on
28 February 1922.

Princess Mary's choice of husband nevertheless came as something of a surprise. This was due in part to the fact that Lord Lascelles at thirty-eight was almost fifteen years older than the Princess, and partly because he was a virtual stranger to the public at large who, in those days, were apt to follow the progress of their princesses more closely than today.

On another note, once the general rejoicing at the wedding had simmered down many people began to ask each other what the Princess saw in her husband. He was not, it was stressed, particularly photogenic, and certainly from available photographs the Viscount, with his thin, rather gaunt features did not add up to everybody's image of a fairy-tale prince charming. Added to that were rumours that Lascelles wasn't, as some put it afterwards, 'quite right'. This wasn't meant as a question mark against his suitability as the Princess's husband, but more directly concerning Lascelles' mental stability. It should be said, however, that this was no more than a rumour; a potentially slanderous snippet of gossip had it been circulated by an identifiable individual. As with all rumours, its reliability was highly questionable. But one thing was quite certain; the idea of being married to the King's only daughter greatly appealed to him and, as the Prince of Wales was supposed to have said at one stage, 'I get commoner and commoner, while Lascelles gets more and more royal.'

No matter what anybody else may have thought, however, Queen Mary was delighted by her daughter's engagement. The King, from a more selfish point of view, was less so. For Princess Mary had always been very close to her father and was, as might be expected of an only daughter, deeply loved by her entire family. When her brothers annoyed their father or fell from grace, for example, it was she who would act as go-between until the rifts were healed. After the wedding, according to Queen Mary, King George completely 'broke down'; and only twenty-four hours later His Majesty noted in his diary, 'I miss darling Mary too awfully.'

For her part, the Princess, like most young princes and princesses of any generation, had caught the popular imagination. She was pretty, lively and, more especially, she managed to do *naturally* all the pleasing things that so many tried to copy without success. Above all, Princess Mary did not consider her rank prevented her from trying to help or give pleasure to others. This was particularly reflected during World War I when she became totally immersed in war work.

One of Princess Mary's first touching ideas was a small gold-coloured tin box on which was stamped her profile flanked by her initial 'M'. Beneath her image read the legend 'Christmas 1914' and around the edges of the lid were stamped the place names: Servia (*sic*), Belgium, France, Japan, Russia. These boxes, which generally contained cigarettes or tobacco, were distributed to the forces together with a postcard photograph of the Princess and a small greetings card which read: 'With best wishes for a Happy Christmas and a Victorous New Year – from the Princess Mary and friends at home'. Sometimes the small gift parcels were accompanied

Princess Mary and Viscount Lascelles in the Throne Room of Buckingham Palace after their wedding.

by photographs of the King and Queen. *Princess Mary's Gift Book*, a special publication, was also produced to raise money for the war.

Princess Mary was seventeen during the world's first year at war and until hostilities ceased in 1918 her programme of war work continued with a growing intensity. She toured hospitals and chatted to the patients, including the severely wounded – the sight of whom would surely have turned any other young woman's stomach – visited munition plants, packed parcels, knitted socks, scarves and other comforts for the troops as well as serving in soup kitchens. The rôle of a royal princess had long ceased to be purely decorative.

In 1918, on her twenty-first birthday, Princess Mary's only request was that she be allowed to work as a probationary nurse at the Hospital for Sick Children at Great Ormond Street. This time her father, who had turned a deaf ear to her previous requests, gave his consent. At this time the Princess had also joined a local Voluntary Aid Detachment and had been appointed by her father to the rank of Colonel-in-Chief of the Royal Scots. So far as she was concerned neither were nominal offices and Princess Mary took both very seriously as she proved at Ypres where, standing among the battle-scarred streets, she reviewed her war-weary troops as they marched past.

Princess Mary was married on 28 February 1922, three years after her father's cousin, Princess Patricia, to whom she had acted as bridesmaid. Yet there were few visible similarities to that first abbey wedding for the simple reason that Mary's was an occasion on the grand scale, with *all* the trappings of royalty. Indeed, as Mabell, Countess of Airlie, recalled, it had been originally planned for the guests to wear full court evening dress including 'feathers and veil' until the Archbishop of Canterbury pronounced the plan too unsuitable for a religious ceremony and there was a mad dash to have other outfits made.

The Princess's brother Bertie, the Duke of York, at that time falling in love with Lady Elizabeth Bowes-Lyon who was to be one of his sister's bridesmaids, wrote enthusiastically to his elder brother David, the Prince of Wales, currently touring India: 'As far as I can make out, the 28th is going to be a day of national rejoicing.' It was. The streets were full once again. Westminster Abbey, from the west door to the high altar, was brimming with guests and hardly a member of the huge Royal Family was absent.

Princess Mary drove with her father from Buckingham Palace in the Irish State Coach and people acclaimed the wedding as the most spectacular royal event since the King's coronation in 1911. A bevy of veiled bridesmaids, including Princess Maud of Fife and Lady May Cambridge, in dresses of silver and white, each clutching a large bouquet of roses attended the 22-year-old bride.

A contemporary description of Princess Mary's gown told observers that it was composed of

silver lamé, veiled with marquisette embroidered in English roses worked with thousands of tiny diamonds and seed pearls in a faint lattice-work design. It was girdled with a silver

Four of Princess Mary's eight bridesmaids. Lady Elizabeth Bowes-Lyon is seen at top right.

BELOW: The Duke of York, Queen Mary, Prince George and Prince Henry after the marriage of Princess Mary.

cord studded with triple rows of pearls and from the left-hand side of the waist hung a trail of orange blossom with silver stems. The train was composed of specially woven white and silver duchess satin, draped with Honiton lace embroidered in baroque pearls, diamonds and silver bullion.

Yet more pearls edged the long net veil which, in turn, was secured by three slim bands of orange blossom, described at the time as a 'tiara'.

The only unscheduled moment of the day came as the Glass Coach, used to transport bride and bridegroom back to Buckingham Palace, halted at the side of the wreath-strewn Cenotaph in Whitehall. Viscount Lascelles saluted and Princess Mary handed her bridal bouquet to an officer on ceremonial duty who, in accordance with her wishes, laid it on the steps of the famous war memorial.

Princess Mary and her husband honeymooned in Shropshire at Weston Park, the Earl of Bradford's rambling estate, before moving into their first home, Goldsborough Hall, near Knaresborough. Seven years later, Lord Lascelles succeeded his father as the sixth Earl of Harewood, and they moved into the magnificent Harewood House. Then, in the 1932 New Year's Honours List, it was announced that King George V had been 'graciously pleased to declare that His Majesty's daughter, Her Royal Highness Princess Victoria Alexandra Alice Mary (Countess of Harewood), shall henceforth bear the style and title of Princess Royal'.

Ostensibly the title is held by Britain's première princess. It is an honour which is only ever bestowed on the eldest daughter of the monarch and Mary became the sixth Princess Royal following the daughters of Charles I, George III, Queen Victoria and Edward VII.

Fourteen months after the Lascelles wedding at Westminster Abbey, there was another; the third to take place there in only four years. This time Princess Mary's elder brother, the Duke of York, second son of George V and the man destined to become King George VI, married Lady Elizabeth Bowes-Lyon, the youngest daughter of the Earl and Countess of Strathmore. The Duke was twenty-seven, his diminutive bride, twenty-two.

Thursday 26 April 1923 dawned wet and overcast. It had rained for most of the previous night and many of the street decorations strung along the wedding route had to remain unfinished right up to the last moment, lest the work should have been washed away. All the same, a million people stood cheek-by-jowl from the gates of Buckingham Palace to the west door of the abbey itself, waiting to cheer the Royal Family and, of course, the bride.

For nearly four hours the abbey bells pealed out over Westminster, and during that time the wedding guests, who had been asked to arrive by ten o'clock, took their seats. Among them was the Prime Minister Mr Bonar Law, Lloyd George, Winston Churchill – who, as happened at the wedding of Princess Elizabeth in 1947, arrived as late as he reasonably could for maximum effect – and the entrancing Lady Diana Cooper. There were boys from the many industrial centres in which the bridegroom had taken such an active interest. Queen Alexandra was accompanied by her sister, the slight but tragic figure of the Dowager Empress Marie Feodorovna, whose son, Tsar Nicholas II, had been butchered with his family in Ekaterinburg some six years earlier.

For the Duke of York, a nervous man afflicted since youth by a speech impediment, his engagement to Lady Elizabeth was something of a personal triumph. The rigours of a royal life had never appealed to this unassuming young woman and she had twice declined the Duke's proposals of marriage. When he mustered the courage to ask again, she agreed to sacrifice both her freedom and her treasured anonymity. In January 1923, the couple travelled down to Sandringham to stay with the King and Queen. Immediately, George V, a strait-laced man who was said to be somewhat averse to the idea of new additions to his family circle, warmed to his future daughter-in-law and Queen Mary, who was equally guilty of not being able to communicate with her children, also fell under the charm of the beguiling Lady Elizabeth.

The following month, the King held a meeting of his Privy Council at Buckingham Palace to give his formal consent to the marriage of his son:

> Now know ye that we have consented ... to the contracting of Matrimony between His Royal Highness Albert Frederick Arthur George, Duke of York, and the Lady Elizabeth Angela Marguerite Bowes-Lyon, youngest daughter of the Right Honourable Claude George, Earl of Strathmore and Kinghorne.

Since weddings always have to be planned to fit in with other official arrangements made for the Royal Family, it was decided that April was the best month. It would be a happy note on which to enter the summer round of royal duties and it would be a suitable prelude to the state visit of the King and Queen to Italy which, it had just been confirmed, would take place early in May.

The Duke of York gave his future Duchess a sapphire engagement ring and from the time the betrothal was made public, gifts began to pour in from every part of the Empire. The Duke of York gave his bride a necklace of diamonds and pearls with a pendant to match, and Lady Elizabeth gave the Duke a dress watch-chain of platinum and pearls.

The bridegroom received a cheque in the region of some two thousand pounds from one organization, which he directed should be spent on entertaining children in areas where unemployment was particularly rife. The Needlemakers' Company sent Lady Elizabeth a thousand needles with gold eyes, the King and Queen gave her an ermine cape and a suite containing a tiara, a necklace and some hair ornaments of diamonds and pale Persian turquoises, a pendant of sapphires and diamonds and a fan of old lace set on a mother-of-pearl frame. The townspeople of Windsor gave the couple a fine grand piano; the City of London contributed some antique silver, and the bridegroom's future mother-in-law, Lady Strathmore, gave the Duke a beautiful miniature of his bride.

Lady Elizabeth chose eight attendants, including Lady May Cambridge, Lady Katharine Hamilton, the Hon. Diamond Hardinge and Lady Mary Thynne, together

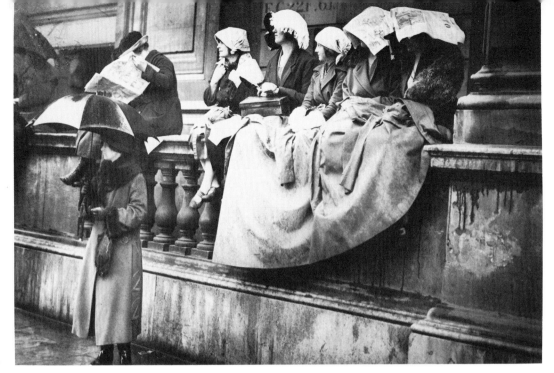

ABOVE: Waiting for the bride. A group of rain-soaked women were among the early arrivals to see the Duke of York and Lady Elizabeth Bowes-Lyon drive past.

BELOW: The Duke and Duchess of York are married at Westminster Abbey on 26 April 1923.

ABOVE: The new Duchess of York returns in the Glass Coach from her wedding.

BELOW: The official wedding group. From left to right, standing: Lady Mary Cambridge, the Duchess of York, the Duke of York, Lady May Cambridge. Seated: the Hon. Diamond Hardinge, Lady Mary Thynne, Lady Katherine Hamilton, Miss Elizabeth Cator. Foreground: the Hon. Elizabeth Elphinstone and the Hon. Cecilia Bowes-Lyon.

with her two young nieces, Cecilia Bowes-Lyon and Elizabeth Elphinstone. The bridegroom chose to be attended by his brother, the Prince of Wales.

A lavish wedding-breakfast was arranged to follow the abbey ceremony; and among the specialities, according to the menu, were *Suprême de Saumon, Reine Mary; Salade Royale* and *Duchess Elizabeth* strawberries. Then the Duke and his bride would leave London for the quiet honeymoon they had planned – first at Polesden Lacey in Surrey and then on to Glamis Castle, the Strathmore family's ancestral home (where, by the way, the unfortunate bride developed whooping-cough).

But before all that, of course, was the wedding itself, and as the members of the Royal Family settled themselves into their carriages for the drive to the abbey, the bride, at her parents' London home, awaited her moment of glory. In those days Bruton Street was a quietly sophisticated off-shoot of Berkeley Square, but today no. 17, the house in which the Strathmores lived, has been swallowed up by the totally characterless premises of a commercial organization.

On that morning in 1923, however, the King's maroon and gold 1902 State landau, drawn by four grey horses and escorted by four mounted policemen, turned into the quiet street and drew up outside the family's home. Already a crowd estimated at between five and six thousand people had gathered at windows, on balconies and in the street itself, and a huge roar of approval filled the air as Lady Elizabeth stepped out of the house.

The Court dressmaker, Madame Handley-Seymour of New Bond Street, had made the bride's simple dress of ivory silk crêpe moiré with its low square neck and short sleeves. A short train was pleated into the back waistband while the front was embroidered with bands of silver lamé enriched with silver thread, pearls and tiny iridescent white beads. The bride's long veil of old *point de Flandres* lace, worn low over the forehead as was the fashion in the 1920s, was loaned by Queen Mary and circling it was a slim wreath of leaves adorned with roses and clusters of orange blossom.

As the landau arrived at Westminster Abbey the sky, as if on cue, miraculously cleared and the sun came out flooding through the church's windows and brightening the interior of the old building. Already carrying a small prayer book, the bride was presented with her wedding bouquet of white roses and heather, and just before starting her long walk along the nave, Lady Elizabeth left her father's side, stepped forward and placed it on the tomb of the Unknown Warrior. The choir began to sing 'Lead Us Heavenly Father, Lead Us', Lady Elizabeth Bowes-Lyon, presently to become Her Royal Highness the Duchess of York, took her father's arm and the bridal procession moved off towards the steps of the sacrarium.

In his address to the bride and bridegroom, the Archbishop of York (who assisted the Archbishop of Canterbury, the Dean of Westminster, the Bishop of London and the Primus of the Episcopalian Church of Scotland) said: 'Will you take and keep this gift of wedded life as a sacred trust? Sacred it must be, for your love and God's love, are within it.... You will have a great ambition to make this one life now given to you something rich, true and beautiful.'

Little did anybody know that day how significant those words would be. Thirteen years later the Prince of Wales, who said that Elizabeth Bowes-Lyon 'brought into the family a lively and refreshing spirit', thrust upon his brother's head the crown he had been born to wear, and the consort's crown on to the head of the reluctant 'little duchess'.

Later in 1923, another royal wedding took place in London, albeit on a much smaller scale. This time the marriage was celebrated at the Chapel Royal, St James's Palace, and while the York wedding had been hailed as 'the wedding of the year', the *other* marriage – for many – relieved the promised monotony of a stark English winter.

In some respects this wasn't a British royal wedding at all because the bridegroom, Crown Prince Gustav Adolf, was Swedish and his bride, Lady Louise Mountbatten, was a daughter of the former Prince Louis of Battenberg. When George V had to change not only the name of the Royal House in 1917 but to re-shuffle some of his relations' titles, Prince Louis became the first Marquess of Milford Haven. His wife, the former Princess Victoria of Hesse (daughter of Queen Victoria's third child, Alice), became the first marchioness and their sons, Princes George and Louis, became the Earl of Medina and Lord Louis Mountbatten respectively.

The wedding took place in England partly at the invitation of the King and partly because the bride and her mother (by now a widow) had made their home in one of the available grace-and-favour apartments at Kensington Palace. It was also in England that Prince Gustav Adolf and Lady Louise's romance had blossomed.

By 1923, Gustav Adolf (who wasn't to become King of Sweden until October 1950) had been a widower for three years. His first wife 'Daisy', Princess Margaret of Connaught (elder daughter of Arthur, Duke of Connaught, and sister of Lady Patricia Ramsay), had died suddenly in 1920 at the age of thirty-eight of erysipelas and blood-poisoning. The Princess, who had done so much and had been so active during the Great War in helping to trace British soldiers who were missing, had been taken prisoner or had been wounded, was greatly mourned. At home in Stockholm were her five children, Gustav Adolf, Sigvard, Bertil, Ingrid (now Queen Mother of Denmark) and Carl Johan.

The Crown Prince's engagement to Louise Mountbatten came as a very great surprise in Sweden therefore, even though it had been widely rumoured in Britain. The Swedish prime minister cabled Stanley Baldwin, his British counterpart. Could he confirm that the Lady Louise was a member of the Royal Family? It might have seemed an odd request in view of England's enlightened stand on the question of royal marriages, but at that time Swedish law did not permit the marriage of the heir to the throne with a commoner. Baldwin replied that the bride was officially considered a member of King George V's family and duly supplied a list showing her precedence at Court.

The Chapel Royal, on that cold, misty morning of 3 November, was ablaze with candle-light. The Archbishop of Canterbury prepared to conduct his second royal marriage of the year and the Lady Louise, in silver and lace, walked slowly through the flower-banked chancel on the arm of her brother, George, attended by her five bridesmaids dressed in apricot chiffon with gold bandanas around their heads.

The wedding-breakfast was held in one of the state rooms at Kensington Palace before the couple left England for a honeymoon in Italy and a triumphant return to Sweden. There they were greeted by thousands of their future subjects who stood in the December drizzle, cheered not only by the sight of their sovereigns-to-be, but by the Christmas lights strung through the barren trees and the abundance of national flags.

There were then to be no royal wedding-bells for some time but, eleven years later – in the summer of 1934 – Prince George, the fourth son of the King and Queen Mary, suddenly made up his mind to fly out to Yugoslavia. Nobody, save his elder brother David, the Prince of Wales, had any idea why he was going, much less an explanation for his impulsive departure. Within forty-eight hours of his arrival at the chalet owned by Prince Paul of Yugoslavia at Bohinj, high in the Julian Alps, however, the Prince's reasons were made clear. For at that time one of Prince Paul's guests was his wife Olga's 27-year-old sister, the exiled Princess Marina.

Marina was tall and dark, as beautiful as she was intelligent, a talented painter and what might be termed today something of a 'culture vulture'. To Prince George she represented everything he would ever look for in a wife. At the age of thirty-two, Prince George already had a naval career behind him. He had retired from the service, with the honorary rank of commander, in 1929, due to a digestive complaint. Before him lay the promise of a life as a roving ambassador.

George was certainly every bit as dashing as his elder brother, the rebel Prince of Wales, and in him was seen something of the extrovert nature of the future Edward VIII, Duke of Windsor. Prince George courted a different kind of press to his brother, whose movements were eagerly followed by the newspaper industry. All the same, Prince George was seen as no less a star in the superficial firmament of the 1930s social whirl; his good looks and personality attracting the notice of both men and women alike. In common with many of his generation Prince George was a keen jazz fan; he loved films as much as he enjoyed dancing, he was adept in field sports and was not averse to a little danger. In fact it is said that, when younger, he shinned up the scaffolding then temporarily encasing Big Ben and, regardless of the risks involved, carried on climbing until he reached the clock's face.

Princess Marina's life by comparison had been far less idealized. She had already experienced the rough with the smooth aspects of the undeniably privileged lot of royalty. One date fêted and adored, the next, as will be seen later on in the case of her uncle Prince Andrew, bombarded with accusations, insults and abuse.

In 1934 she and her parents, Prince and Princess Nicholas of Greece, had entered the eleventh year of exile from their homeland. They lived quietly and, of necessity, modestly, in an apartment on the Avenue Henri Martin in Paris, from where her father, hitherto Greece's foremost royal patron of the arts, worked as a painter. His wife, formerly the Grand Duchess Helen of Russia, worked in a home for Russian

ABOVE: Prince Gustav Adolf's first wedding took place on 15 June 1905. With the prince is his bride, Princess Margaret of Connaught, and her attendants.

BELOW: Following his wife's death in 1920, Prince Gustav Adolf took as his second wife Lady Louise Mountbatten on 3 November 1923.

refugee and orphaned children, which she established at St Germain from the proceeds of the sale of some of her mother's jewellery.

In the meantime, however, George and Marina, as with every couple in love, briefly inhabited a very private, insular world; and the changes that were to affect the Britain of the mid-1930s were far from their minds that summer. All the same, the reign of King George V was gradually drawing to a close; the overture of the greatest constitutional blockbuster of the century had already begun, and even more ominously, the country was steadily drifting in the direction of a second and even more devastating world war.

But for now, George and Marina were the focus of attention as their engagement delighted the world. At Bohinj they were heaped with flowers by local villagers in national costume; they returned to Paris to be greeted by delirious crowds and personalities who suddenly, and conveniently, recalled that they knew the family of exiled royalties in their midst; in London, public excitement hit fever-pitch. Not since an earlier Viking princess, Marina's great-aunt Alexandra of Denmark, had set foot on British soil in 1862 to marry the future Edward VII, had a foreign princess been welcomed so enthusiastically.

Part of Marina's appeal was undoubtedly her 'Englishness'. Her father had been taught from boyhood by his own father, King George I of Greece, that as a royal prince he must never expect to escape or neglect his obligations or ask for favours. The privilege of royal birth, he maintained, was to be of service to others. They were lessons Prince Nicholas was never to forget, and these same principles were instilled into his children. In turn they were drummed into their own sons and daughters.

Marina had also been cared for by an English governess so that the country and its customs were, in effect, second nature to her. In David Duff's book *Hessian Tapestry* he wrote that:

Marina even prayed in English. When asked by Queen Olga [her paternal grandmother] why she did not do so in Greek, she replied: 'I have arranged it with God. I told Him I liked to talk to Him in English best, and He said: "Please yourself, Marina."'

Fact or fiction it is hard to know since Grace Ellison, probably the first of the Princess's biographers and a friend of the family, stated in her own book in 1934 that the Princess said her prayers in Greek and the Lord's Prayer in English. Either way it is not significant, except to show the affinity she already had with the country that was to become her own.

In more general terms, Princess Marina, during the 1930s and 1940s, proved to be the one royal female capable of setting a trend in fashion: the style or angle of a hat, the line of a dress, the fabric of a ballgown. She invariably looked like a *Vogue* fashionplate and those who could afford to followed her lead. At one point a hat or an outfit in 'Marina blue' became *de rigueur* for fashion-conscious young women.

Three weeks prior to the wedding, the Prince, supported by his elder brothers, made his appearance before the House of Lords. The King had created his son Baron

Downpatrick, Earl of St Andrews and Duke of Kent. Not since the lifetime of Queen Victoria's father had there been a Duke of Kent even if some contemporary writers seem to overlook the fact that George was not the first. The newly created peer duly took his place on 7 November.

The wedding of Prince George and Princess Marina was arranged to take place at Westminster Abbey on the morning of 29 November 1934. The abbey ceremony would, of course, follow the rites of the established English Church, but upon the couple's return to Buckingham Palace a second marriage service would be observed in the private chapel, this time according to the ancient ritual of the Greek Orthodox Church to which the Princess belonged.

The Kent wedding was the first in the abbey since 1923, and it was designed to follow much the same lines as before. The Prince of Wales would act as his brother's best man and the eight bridesmaids, five of them princesses, were: Princess Elizabeth of York (the present Queen), the Princesses Irene, Eugenie and Katherine of Greece, Princess Juliana (now Queen) of the Netherlands, the Grand Duchess Kira of Russia, Lady Mary Cambridge and Lady Iris Mountbatten.

With the marriages of his brothers, the Prince of Wales must undoubtedly have been made acutely aware of his own responsibilities. In 1934 his relationship with the woman on whom the entire nation was so soon to vent its spleen had already gathered momentum. The Prince of Wales's romantic liaisons had always given rise to a certain amount of gossip but none more so than his involvement with Mrs Wallis Simpson, the twice-married, handsome American whom he had met through his previous love, Lady Furness.

Life for his brothers must have appeared painfully straightforward. Albert, Duke of York, married for eleven years by now, had established a comfortable family life at 145 Piccadilly; George stood on the brink of marrying the loveliest princess in all Europe; and next on the list of proud bridegrooms was Henry, Duke of Glou-cester, already a dedicated soldier and in love with Lady Alice Montagu-Douglas-Scott, the daughter of the Duke of Buccleuch. It was not surprising that the Prince of Wales should ask his brother to add Mrs Simpson's name to the list of personal wedding guests. She wasn't allocated a place among the visiting royalty, needless to say, but it gave the Prince of Wales some pleasure to know that she was in the abbey.

Princess Marina was yet another silver-clad bride. The morning of 29 November was typically frosty; the streets filled with crowds typical of such an occasion to whom the bride, as she drove in the state landau to the abbey, must have resembled some form of snow queen.

The man to whom was entrusted the job of creating the year's most talked-about bridal gown was Captain Edward Molyneux, to whom the Princess had gone for most of her outfits in the past. The bride had consulted him at his Paris salon, where the design and the fabric were chosen. It was an arrangement that suited Molyneux

The Duke and Duchesss of Kent in the Throne Room of Buckingham Palace. In this group they are seen with King George v and Queen Mary and royal relations from four countries: Denmark, Greece, Norway and Yugoslavia.

LEFT: Prince George and Princess Marina pose for an official wedding portrait.

and Princess Marina well enough, for she had not yet left her parents' home for London. The designer had salons in both the French and English capitals, which meant that while the material could be woven in Lyons the gown itself would be made at Molyneux's Grosvenor Street establishment. Unlike other wedding-dresses, however, Princess Marina's would have to be made in two weeks. The reason for this was simple enough. The material, a delicate white and silver brocade embodying in its design the English rose, was considered too fragile to be brought across the Channel earlier than was necessary only to be left lying around in a storeroom. So from the factory in France it found its way to London via Paris and in Grosvenor Street a team of seamstresses set to work. Included in their numbers were a group of Russian refugees, employed at the Princess's request because she felt the gesture would illustrate her sympathy with all those whose lives had been uprooted by the revolution in her mother's country only seventeen years earlier.

London's main thoroughfares were decorated in celebration and at night illuminated for the sightseers. Union Jacks and the Greek national flags fluttered side by side; overhead bunting helped secure giant coloured bells and the union of the ruling British royal house with that of the exiled Greek royal dynasty was further symbolized by intertwined crowns.

On the morning of the wedding, while the bride was dressing at Buckingham Palace, the bridegroom left his York House apartment to cash a cheque at a nearby bank as many a bridegroom must have done before and since. Too little cash wouldn't augur well on such an important occasion. To the protests that he could surely have sent somebody else, the young Duke replied that it had given him something to do.

By mid-morning London had donned the full panoply of a royal wedding. British and Greek royalty had assembled at Westminster Abbey, facing each other across the wide sacrarium. Seated on either side of the nave were ambassadors, high commissioners, various foreign emissaries, church representatives, members of parliament, representatives of the armed forces, peers and peeresses, friends and acquaintances and, adding to the majesty of the scene, the Gentlemen-at-Arms in scarlet uniforms clutching their ceremonial pikes. The bridegroom in full naval uniform arrived with the Prince of Wales, the organ filled the abbey with sound, the bells performed their staggering concerto of no less than five thousand changes and the trumpeters waited to sound the fanfare that would announce the arrival of the bride. The attendants arrived; the procession of officiating clergy, including the head of the Greek Orthodox Church in London, formed, led by the Archbishop of Canterbury, Dr Cosmo Lang, who was to perform the marriage ceremony.

At last came the bride in her slim sheath-like gown with its draped neckline and long tight sleeves. On her head she wore a magnificent fringe tiara – the gift of the City of London – from which flowed her long white tulle veil with a train which widened at the bottom to ten feet. One hand rested on the arm of her distinguished-looking father, Prince Nicholas; the other held her bouquet of lilies.

The Archbishop in his address referred to the Duke of Kent's place in his family when he said: 'You, sir, have already ... taken your place in the service of the community . . .' and he referred to the new Duchess of Kent as 'you, dear bride', when he reminded her of the position she was now to hold, 'in ministering to the needs of the good British folk', who, the Archbishop told her, 'have already, with a warmth so swift and spontaneous, taken you into their hearts'.

With the Church of England ceremony over, the bride and bridegroom returned to Buckingham Palace in the Glass Coach – so called because of its large windows – for the Greek wedding ceremony in the palace's private chapel. That ceremony, celebrated by Archbishop Strinopoulos Germanos, composed of ancient Greek and Roman customs, was the first double ceremony to be held for over half a century. The last time was the marriage in St Petersburg of Queen Victoria's son Prince Alfred, Duke of Edinburgh, to Grand Duchess Marie, daughter of Tsar Alexander II, an aunt of Princess Marina's mother.

The wedding-breakfast in the Ball-Supper Room followed this ancient ceremony and then it was time for the bride and groom to take their leave. The first part of their honeymoon was spent in Staffordshire at Himley Hall, the home of the Earl of Dudley. The Kents then moved on to Trent Park near Barnet, owned by Sir Philip Sassoon. Following a family Christmas at Sandringham, the honeymoon culminated in a cruise to the West Indies during which they met, and established a very firm friendship with, America's President Roosevelt, thus forging another link between Britain and the United States and adding immeasurably to the goodwill which existed between the two nations.

Almost a year later the private chapel at Buckingham Palace was to be the scene for another royal wedding; this time between Prince Henry, Duke of Gloucester, the third son of the King and Queen, and Lady Alice Montagu-Douglas-Scott, the third daughter of the seventh Duke of Buccleuch. Originally the wedding had been arranged to take place at Westminster Abbey, but when the bride's father died unexpectedly only weeks before the wedding-day it was decided, out of respect, to celebrate the marriage on a much smaller and quieter scale. Thus, the abbey ceremony was cancelled and plans were hastily rearranged.

Prince Henry, born on 31 March 1900, ten months before the death of his great-grandmother, Queen Victoria – whom he had been taken to see at Osborne during the summer of that year – had known Lady Alice for some time. In fact she had been among the bridesmaids at the wedding of his cousin, Lady May Cambridge, to Captain Henry Abel Smith in October 1931. (This was also the occasion on which the little Princess Elizabeth of York made her début in the rôle of bridesmaid.)

The Buccleuchs, needless to say, were not without their royal connections. The seventh Duke had been a friend of the King since childhood, and Lady Alice's elder sister, Margaret, known to her family as 'Mida', had been appointed a lady-in-waiting to Princess Alice, Countess of Athlone. Later, the Princess was to stand as godmother to Lady Margaret's daughter, Anne.

On the day of the royal wedding – 6 November 1935 – the chapel at Buckingham Palace was bedecked with flowers and lighted tapers; and although it was strictly the Royal Family's *private* chapel, its dimensions may easily be judged today since it is now open to the public as The Queen's Gallery.

From her family's Mayfair home, Lady Alice drove to Buckingham Palace in the Glass Coach. This was a reversal of the normal procedure, since the Glass Coach in the 1920s and 1930s was reserved only for the return journey of royal bride and bridegroom. On this occasion, however, fewer still would have been able to catch a glimpse of the bride had she travelled in a closed landau, as there was to be no return procession.

Upon her arrival at the palace, Lady Alice, wearing a long gown of palest pink satin with a full tulle veil to match, made her way to the chapel attended by her eight bridesmaids: Princess Elizabeth and her five-year-old sister, Margaret Rose, Lady Mary Cambridge, Miss Anne Hawkins, Miss Claire Phipps, Lady Elizabeth Scott, Lady Angela Scott and Miss Moyra Scott. As she entered to the sound of the choir, Prince Henry, dressed in his gold-braided uniform of the 10th Royal Hussars, turned to greet her.

The Archbishop of Canterbury married them, and in little more than an hour the new Duke and Duchess of Gloucester were standing on the palace's balcony acknowledging the greetings of the crowds gathered in the street below.

One year later, the pattern of events in the life of the British Royal Family had changed considerably. George V was dead, the Prince of Wales was King, and the full saga of his relationship with Mrs Simpson, which had long been common knowledge on the other side of the Atlantic and throughout Europe, finally broke through the floodgates of Fleet Street, swamping the newspapers with endless speculation of what was to come.

Ernest Simpson, a quiet, dapper businessman, agreed to the divorce his wife pressed for while eminent courtiers asked whether the end of one marriage signalled the start of another. Moment by moment the drama that was to end in abdication built up.

After innumerable books on the subject, however, including both principal players' autobiographies, a film, a stage play and a television series, the story of Edward VIII and Mrs Simpson needs no further explanation or embellishment.

Few saw the departure of the ex-King from the country over which he had ruled so briefly. Little more than twenty-four hours after he had signed the Instrument of Abdication at Fort Belvedere, his private estate in Windsor Great Park, an un-marked limousine sped out of the gates bound for Portsmouth. From there at two o'clock on the morning of Saturday 12 December 1936, the destroyer *Fury* slipped anchor bound for Boulogne; on board was its royal passenger. He left behind him a family harbouring feelings of bitterness as well as hope, and a nation divided too in their feelings towards the man on whom, as King, they had pinned their hopes for the future.

Five months later, after a separation almost as agonizing as the events of the past

ABOVE: Following their marriage on 6 November 1935, Prince Henry, Duke of Gloucester, and his bride, Lady Alice Montagu-Douglas-Scott, wave from the balcony of Buckingham Palace. With them are Princess Elizabeth, King George V, Princess Margaret, the Princess Royal and Queen Mary.

BELOW: The Duke and Duchess of Gloucester after their wedding in the private chapel at Buckingham Palace. From left to right, back row: Miss Claire Phipps, the Duke of York, Lady Elizabeth Scott, Lady Angela Scott, the Prince of Wales, Miss Moira Scott. Front row: Lady Mary Cambridge, Princess Elizabeth, Princess Margaret and Miss Anne Hawkins.

year themselves, the ex-King joined Mrs Simpson at the château de Candé, Tours, put at their disposal by a sympathetic French industrialist.

In London, preparations for the coronation of the new king, George VI, and his consort were nearing completion. It had been decided not to alter the date originally arranged for the coronation of Edward VIII and so it remained set for 12 May. Nine days earlier, Mrs Simpson learned from England that her divorce from her second husband had been made final, and so, at last, plans could go ahead for her third wedding.

Both the newly created Duke of Windsor and Mrs Simpson hoped for a quiet wedding. The château de Candé was an ideal setting and apart from the press men who had faithfully pursued the Duke and his wife-to-be for months, the nightmare of dense crowds descending on the isolated castle, anxious to witness history in the making, receded. Few, if any, would be prepared to negotiate the narrow wooded paths of the Loire valley snaking around the picturesque château. Only those directly involved would make the trek.

At last the date for the wedding was finalized, and 3 June 1937 dawned an idyllic day, warm and sunny. The only thing which marred his wedding-day for the Duke was the absence of any members of his family. Foolishly he had hoped for the presence of his sister Mary, who, unmoved in the face of her disillusioned relations, had remained sympathetic during those critical days in England. Even wilder was his hope that Queen Mary might attend the ceremony. While he would never lose her love on a purely personal level, her 'official' attitude on the subject remained unchanged. David, as he was still known to his family, had put pleasure before duty and in the world of royalty that was a cardinal sin which was unforgivable. So far as Wallis Simpson was concerned, Queen Mary totally disregarded her existence and it wasn't until many years later that the Queen could even bring herself to mention her son's wife in her correspondence. Even then it was never more than: 'I send a kind message to your wife.'

The 'velvet and ermine curtain', of which the Duchess of Windsor figuratively spoke in her memoirs, may have fallen but not everybody at home felt cheated. Shortly before the wedding a message was received that the Rev. R. Anderson Jardine, vicar of St Paul's church, Darlington, had offered his ecclesiastical services and, in defiance of his bishop, had made it known that he would be happy to travel to France and perform the marriage ceremony. His offer, after due investigation, was accepted and on 2 June Mr Jardine arrived at the château. Cecil Beaton, a great admirer of Mrs Simpson's, also arrived that day to take the official wedding photographs; so did Mrs Constance Spry, who was to be responsible for arranging all the flowers at the express wish of the bride. 'This was her wedding present to me,' the Duchess later recalled.

A civil ceremony, as is the custom on the Continent, preceded the religious service which was held in the château's music room. A handful of newspaper reporters were allowed in to cover the wedding and various French dignitaries and their wives also received invitations. But of their own guests – personal friends of long standing –

The wedding of the Duke and Duchess of Windsor was celebrated on 3 June 1937 at the château de Candé.

there were only eight: 'Fruity' Metcalfe, the Duke's former equerry, who was to act as best man; Lady Alexandra Metcalfe; Herman and Katherine Rogers, fellow Americans who had never left Wallis Simpson's side; Randolph Churchill, son of Sir Winston; Walter Monckton (who had borne the news that the Duke's bride was not to share her husband's title of Royal Highness – by order of King George VI); and Eugene and Kitty de Rothschild.

Mrs Simpson, dressed by Mainbocher, in a long, elegant gown of pale blue crêpe satin with a small veiled hat of feathers to match, entered on the arm of Herman Rogers. 'Fruity' Metcalfe slipped the bridegroom the prayer book which Queen Mary had given to him as a boy, and the Rev. R. Anderson Jardine quietly performed what was arguably the most historic and emotionally charged royal wedding of the century. Lady Alexandra Metcalfe noted after the ceremony that: 'It was hard not to cry and in fact I did.' The new Duchess of Windsor put on a brave face even though the Duke, as had been known to happen in the past, gave emotion its head and, according to Lady Alexandra: 'He had tears running down his face when he came into the salon after the ceremony.'

The following day the couple received a telegram from the King and Queen, followed by another from Queen Mary, and that evening the Windsors left the château de Candé for Austria, where they spent most of that summer at Count Munster's manor house, Wasserleonburg.

In the years that followed the Duke of Windsor seemed only to visit Great Britain on the most pitiful of occasions – the funerals of his royal relations. He did, of course, visit frequently enough in a private and unofficial capacity but invitations were never extended for the more joyous of family events. The Duchess of Windsor rarely accompanied her husband. She was, however, officially received by the Royal Family for the first time four days after her thirtieth wedding anniversary when, on 7 June 1967, together with her husband, the present Queen invited them both to attend the unveiling of a memorial plaque to the Duke's mother, Queen Mary. On that occasion, the Duke was given precedence immediately after Queen Elizabeth the Queen Mother, but before his only surviving brother, the Duke of Gloucester, and other more junior members of the Royal Family.

Five years later, in June 1972, the Duchess of Windsor returned to England and, at the Queen's invitation, spent three days as her guest at Buckingham Palace. But this visit was not a happy one: the Duchess had come to bury her husband.

5
The New Elizabethan Age

From the time of Princess Elizabeth's birth in 1926, Queen Mary, her wise and revered grandmother, had harboured an inkling that she might one day become Queen. The possibilities were remote, but nonetheless real. The abdication of Edward VIII meant, of course, that the new King's eldest daughter – ten years old at the time – was no longer simply the Princess Elizabeth of York, but heiress presumptive to the throne of England. From that moment, her life at Court assumed a new and even greater significance. It also meant that the country as a whole would take a deeper interest in her development from a fair-haired child to a poised young woman about to make her début in society. Her friends too would be scrutinized as she grew older – especially by the press – for any signs of a burgeoning romance. But it was not until 1946 that the outside world caught its first discreet glimmer of a love that resulted in the Princess's wedding on a bleak November day in 1947, described by Winston Churchill as, 'A flash of colour on the hard road we have to travel.'

The Second World War had ended only two years before and Britain still nursed her battle scars. The winter of 1946–7 had been particularly bitter, made even colder by continued rationing. India gained her independence, and the British Empire began to change into the British Commonwealth we know today. The whole of Europe began the long, costly process of pulling itself together again.

With the country in despondent mood, it wasn't surprising that few dissenting voices were to be heard when Princess Elizabeth's engagement to the former Prince Philip of Greece was made public. But not everybody was happy about the choice of bridegroom. The left-wing press made great play of Philip's foreign origin, and in one opinion poll taken at the time, forty per cent of those asked were opposed to the marriage for the same reason. The xenophobia which still gripped Britain meant that the Prince was regarded if not with any real animosity, then certainly with suspicion. Nonetheless, love triumphed over politics and jubilant crowds danced in the streets.

The promised wedding would be the first major royal event since the coronation of King George VI and Queen Elizabeth in 1937, and as Walter Bagehot, the foremost Victorian exponent on the British Constitution, had written in the 1870s, 'A princely

marriage is the brilliant edition of a universal fact and as such it rivets mankind'
– a maxim particularly pertinent in this instance.

Princess Elizabeth was thirteen when she first met her future husband at Dartmouth
just before the outbreak of war, and although the young prince may not have taken
a great deal of notice of her then, their feelings towards one another had grown
immeasurably in the following years.

Throughout 1946, Princess Elizabeth, giving emotion its head, had been unable
to speak of anything but 'Philip'. It was 'Philip this' and 'Philip that', and Queen
Elizabeth, among the first to realize what had developed between her daughter and
the tall, good-looking son of Prince and Princess Andrew of Greece, gently suggested
that the photograph of a fresh-faced, clean-shaven 'Philip' currently on display in
her daughter's private sitting-room might be giving too much away too soon. The
Princess appreciated her mother's point, but rather than remove her sweetheart's
image altogether, she merely exchanged one study for another – this time showing
a smiling sailor prince, his face masked by a full bushy beard. Not very convincing
perhaps, but then how does a twenty-year-old, already besotted, disguise the fact
that she is hopelessly in love?

By the end of the year, the American press had already marked Prince Philip as
Elizabeth's future husband. But even they were five years behind one even more
astute observer, Sir Henry 'Chips' Channon. To be fair, however, Channon was
closer to royalty on a personal level than any American journalist. At a cocktail party
in January 1941 'Chips' met Philip of Greece who was, he noted, 'extraordinarily
handsome'. Sir Henry's diary entry for that day went further: 'He [Philip] is to be
our prince consort, and that is why he is serving in our Navy. He is charming, but
I deplore such a marriage; he and Princess Elizabeth are too interrelated.'

But all over Europe the press, while rating Philip as one of the most eligible suitors,
half-heartedly continued to speculate, linking the Princess's name with some very
unlikely 'husbands-to-be'. Among them was the Regent Prince Charles of Belgium,
added to the list because it was said he was on the point of marrying an English
princess. What the press tended to overlook, presumably as incidental, was the age
difference: the Belgian prince was already forty-one. Yet while Fleet Street and its
European brethren continued to play its game of cat and mouse, Philip was discreetly
paying court to the Princess. He frequently visited the Royal Family when on leave
from the Navy or when stationed at the *Royal Arthur* Naval Shore Base at Corsham
in Wiltshire.

It was also convenient that Philip's uncle, Lord Louis Mountbatten, lived very
near Buckingham Palace, so long as discretion remained the better part of valour.
And for them both, the lessons in diplomacy they had had to learn paid off. Not
once could any eagle-eyed observer say they had seen the Prince and Princess alone
together. On the contrary, when Philip escorted Princess Elizabeth to various private
soirées, they always went under cover of a group of close friends and were never
to be seen paying undue attention to one another.

Framed by a billowing white ensign, the view from Admiralty Arch as Princess Elizabeth's procession made its way down the Mall towards Westminster Abbey. Crowd density is especially evident in this photograph.

It was a ruse that worked perfectly, but before the world could be informed that the Princess had already chosen her future consort, there was the Royal Family's long-standing visit to South Africa, an arduous ten-week tour of duty undertaken at the Government's insistence, despite some ill-informed criticism at home about the timing of the visit. Whilst there, Princess Elizabeth celebrated her twenty-first birthday at Cape Town and from Government House on 21 April 1947 pledged her life to the service of the 'Great Imperial Commonwealth...'

In London meanwhile, the question of Philip's naturalization, which had been under discussion since the autumn of 1944, was settled. It had been a seemingly endless process, the ramifications of which had to be patiently borne if Philip, according to Admiralty regulations, wanted to receive a permanent commission in the Royal Navy which, of course, he did. He had already proved himself an outstanding cadet at Dartmouth, having won the King's Dirk, and an even more worthy and astute officer in action, being mentioned in dispatches during the battle of Cape Matapan. 'Thanks to his alertness and appreciation of the situation,' commended his captain on board the battleship *Valiant*, 'we were able to sink in five minutes two eight-inch gun Italian cruisers.' In the spring of 1945, George VI raised the matter with the Home Office. The Home Secretary, Mr Chuter Ede, conferred with the Prime Minister and the Secretary of State for Foreign Affairs and the Kings of both England and Greece were required to signify their approval to the proposal. The main problem now – and the reason why any decision was further delayed – was that the Greek crown was going through one of its many phases of instability and the Prince's permanent 'defection' to Great Britain, no matter on what grounds, might be taken as a bad reflection on the future of the Greek monarchy.

Eventually, the difficulties in the Aegean were resolved. A plebiscite was held, the crown restored, and Philip was able to surrender his rank and titles as a Prince of the Royal Houses of Greece and Denmark with impunity. On 18 March 1947, Philip's naturalization was announced in the *London Gazette*, listing the former Prince simply as Lieutenant Philip Mountbatten, RN. After a good deal of discussion it was determined that Philip should adopt the anglicized version of his mother's name, Battenberg. The name had, in fact, been translated to Mountbatten in 1917, when King George V commanded that all German titles be dropped due to hostilities during World War I.

All this had, not unnaturally, given an added boost to the popular belief that an engagement between Philip and Princess Elizabeth was imminent. What the public at this time had no way of knowing, however, was that the official denials from Buckingham Palace were issued in deadly earnest. King George VI wouldn't, or couldn't, accept that his elder daughter had actually fallen madly in love with the first young man she had ever met. His concern was two-fold: it wasn't simply the concern of a father that his dearly loved daughter was sure of her own mind, but also the concern of a King needing to reassure himself that the heir to his throne hadn't let her heart rule her head in her choice of consort.

In 1945, the King had written to his mother, the Dowager Queen Mary, that he and the Queen felt Elizabeth was still too young for marriage. At the beginning of 1947 it was only just beginning to dawn on him that Elizabeth and Philip really did know what they wanted. There was never any doubt, however, as to King George's feelings towards the object of his daughter's affections. 'I like Philip,' he wrote; 'he is intelligent, has a good sense of humour and thinks about things in the right way.' And Philip, although he may not have been aware of it at the time, had earned full marks from his prospective father-in-law, when, having just dispensed with his own titles, he politely turned down His Majesty's offer of British royal status – at least for the time being. To Philip, titles meant very little. Indeed, his father, Prince Andrew of Greece, had come perilously near to death because of his own.

In the wake of World War I, during which Prince Andrew's brother, King Constantine, clung desperately to neutrality, despite heavy intimidation on the part of both the enemy and the allies, peace returned to Greece. Constantine, who had been forced to abdicate in June 1917, handing over the throne to his reluctant successor (his son Alexander), was eventually invited to return after his son died from blood-poisoning. The exiled monarch cautiously replied that his return to the country he loved would depend totally upon the result of a plebiscite, which he insisted be called to determine the true feelings of the nation. The votes counted revealed that only 10,883 voters from a total of over one million were against the King's return.

This second honeymoon was, however, destined to be brief; among the many problems Constantine returned to was the legacy of war with Turkey, which erupted during the summer of 1921. The Greeks were ill-trained and woefully equipped; the Turks were not. The situation led Greece to insurrection and revolution and the officers, whose loyalty was questionable, demanded once more that the King abdicate, this time in favour of his son Prince George. The King's family were told they could remain, but the monarch himself, broken both in health and spirit, had to leave to face a life of exile once more. He died two years later in January 1923 at Palermo.

The drama surrounding Prince Andrew's arrest on the island of Corfu was about to be enacted. In October, the Prince received a summons – more of a command than a request – to go to Athens and act as a witness giving evidence at the trials of former ministers accused of having instigated past hostilities. Andrew complied with orders, only to discover that he had fallen into a trap and it was he who was to stand trial before the revolutionaries charged with military incompetence. The Prince realized only too well that he stood no more than a few steps away from a firing squad.

It was only the strenuous efforts of his family which caused the Prince's life to be spared. His wife, Princess Alice, sent appeals to every European head of state; Queen Sophie, wife of the deposed King Constantine, appealed directly to King George V of England, the French president and the King of Spain; whilst Princess Nicholas, Andrew's sister-in-law (and the mother of the late Princess Marina, incidentally), succeeded in her appeal to the Pope. All those approached sent their representatives post-haste to Athens. The English King took his willingness to assist one step further and, as well as an emissary, ordered the cruiser *Calypso* to enter the Greek port of Phaleron.

On 2 December the sentence was passed: Prince Andrew was to be exiled from his country for life, and he and his family left Greece aboard the *Calypso*.

Although only six months old when all this took place, it was, in all probability, an episode the young Philip heard spoken about occasionally as he grew up in Paris, and it is also probably true to say that few sailors had been introduced to Britain's Royal Navy quite so young or under such exceptional circumstances.

At twenty-six, however, all that mattered to Philip was his own career in the service that had saved his father's life, and the fact that he was in love with a king's daughter. Yet even so, any announcement of his engagement to Princess Elizabeth would still have to hang fire. The King and Queen with their daughters were not due home from South Africa until the end of April, and since King George had yet to give his formal consent to the marriage, the timing of *any* announcement was far from certain. By July, the King, having overcome his natural fear of losing his daughter in marriage, approved the betrothal at a meeting of the Privy Council and he and the Queen were able to tell the world on 10 July that their 'dearly beloved daughter' was to be married.

News of the engagement made headlines if not in every corner of the globe then certainly throughout the English-speaking countries; the British press only allowed just enough room for an assortment of other news items on its front pages between copious pictures of Princess Elizabeth arriving for a private dance at Apsley House the night before the announcement, her engagement ring of diamonds, and broad hints that the honeymoon might well be spent in Canada.

On 11 July, the *Daily Express* leader column told its readers that: 'The announcement of the betrothal of Princess Elizabeth and Lieutenant Mountbatten heightens the ordinary man's sense of history. It enables him to project the past into the future and to see the rich pattern of events.' The leader went on to remind readers not only of the love-match between Queen Victoria and Prince Albert, with whom comparisons were inevitable, but also of the Princess's illustrious namesake, the first Queen Elizabeth. The article concluded with a timely message of hope, similar to those which were to fill countless columns at the beginning of the new reign some five years later: 'This age into which Princess Elizabeth was born contains no dream of El Dorado such as inspired the Tudor sea-dogs and the Victorian pioneers. Instead, it has been filled with the nightmare of violent change [and] of misery in the world on a scale unimagined before....' Riding high on hopes that Britain would regain her slowly crumbling supremacy in all things, the national press heaped countless similar eulogies upon the bride of 1947.

Yet if Britain was destined to lose her foothold as a leading world power, the British themselves, in great need of a morale booster at this time, seized upon the royal wedding as being just that: an opportunity to fly the flag again and hold aloft the one symbol of unity for all the world to see.

Her Royal Highness the Bride.

On the afternoon that the engagement became official, Elizabeth and Philip appeared in public together, ostensibly for the first time. The occasion was one of the season's royal garden parties in the grounds of Buckingham Palace, after which they drove the short distance along the Mall to Marlborough House. There they were received by an ecstatic Queen Mary, who, at the age of eighty, delighted in the knowledge that her granddaughter's marriage would rekindle the links forged abroad by Queen Victoria and her immediate descendants during the closing years of the previous century. Indeed, not only were Princess Elizabeth and Philip third cousins through their joint descent from the great Queen herself – Elizabeth through the line of Edward VII, and Philip through Princess Alice of Hesse – but they were also cousins through the line of King Christian IX of Denmark. It was all very impressive, but the British public were more concerned with flocking round Buckingham Palace to cheer their future sovereign, than with a directory of her royal predecessors, no matter how fascinating they may have been.

By the time Buckingham Palace told the media that Princess Elizabeth and her fiancé were to be married at Westminster Abbey on 20 November – despite stories that George VI would have preferred a spring wedding for his daughter – the many departments of the Royal Household had been swung into feverish action. The Army was making plans for its ceremonial manœuvres; His Majesty's printers were busy preparing the embossed invitation cards; and Norman Hartnell, the royal fashion designer, was busily creating several designs for the outfits to be worn by the various royal ladies. To a less talented dressmaker such an occasion would have been at best forbidding. But Hartnell, used to the stresses of more than forty years of royal patronage, took his special commission calmly. In 1935 he had designed the pearl pink satin gown worn by Lady Alice Montagu-Douglas-Scott for her wedding to Princess Elizabeth's uncle, the Duke of Gloucester; an earlier bridal robe for the Marchioness of Bath had been hailed as 'the eighth wonder of the world'; and for the Coronation of the King and Queen, Hartnell had designed the slim white satin dresses worn by the Queen's six maids-of-honour.

All those gowns had, however, been made during the years separating the two world wars, years that were unhampered by rationing laws. But notwithstanding such drawbacks, a true craftsman is always able to make the most of what he has to hand and Princess Elizabeth, for her part, had been saving her clothing coupons for her bridal attire. Royalty and commoners were obliged to abide by the rules of the day, though in common with any other young woman on the verge of matrimony, the Princess received an extra two hundred coupons as a government contribution towards her trousseau. At the same time many loyal and sympathetic female admirers had made their contribution to swell the bride's dress allowance by sending her some of their own coupons. This spontaneous gesture deeply moved the Princess, who attached a personal note of thanks to them all before they were returned to their rightful owners. It was, as many will remember, illegal to give away clothing coupons – even to a future queen. On the other hand, to all those who had sent Princess Elizabeth pairs of nylon stockings, another note of thanks was delivered. In this in-

The marriage of Princess Elizabeth and the Duke of Edinburgh is solemnized at Westminster Abbey,
20 November 1947.

stance the Princess felt that it would have been discourteous not to have accepted them in the spirit in which they were sent, and then as now she was particularly anxious not to give offence.

Meanwhile, with the material 'purchased' from the Princess's clothing coupons, Hartnell was able to create the type of gown most of Elizabeth's young contemporaries dreamed of. Later, when the chosen fabric had been publicized, certain liverish voices were quick to demand the 'nationality' of the silkworms, anxious lest they should have been provided by 'enemy' territories such as Japan or Italy. In the event it was confirmed that the potentially explosive larvæ had been supplied by China.

During the weeks immediately preceding the wedding, gifts from far and wide arrived in London and were exhibited at St James's Palace. The useful and the purely decorative were displayed side by side. From the South African ostrich farmers came a cape of feathers for the Princess, and the promise of a thousand blankets from Montevideo for the poor children of London. The Girl Guides Association gave an eighteenth-century Carlton House writing table, selected by the bride herself; the American ambassador in London gave a beautiful set of Steuben crystal plates engraved with pictures after the famous naturalist Audubon; from Italy came a set of eighteenth-century Dresden chocolate cups and saucers from Pope Pius XII, and a splendid seventeenth-century carved oak chest containing nineteen pieces of specially woven Italian silk, presented by the president of the republic. Nearer home again, the Elizabeths, Alexandras and Marys of the borough of Twickenham sent an inscribed Georgian silver fruit basket. Jewels – notably diamonds, rubies and sapphires, were presented in abundance. The Nizam of Hyderabad, possibly the greatest friend Britain had among the Indian princes, sent Princess Elizabeth a diamond tiara with matching necklace; from the people of Burma a necklace containing ninety-six rubies; and from the Lord Mayor, the Bank of England clearing banks and other prominent City of London interests, a magnificent 'sunburst' diamond necklace.

Queen Mary gave her granddaughter nine pieces of jewellery from her own private collection, including a priceless diamond tiara (which the Queen, as she now is, of course, wears most often); and from the King and Queen, among other items, two necklaces – one of fifty and the other of forty-six graduated pearls.

But the most humble of gifts, and one of the most touching, came from Mahatma Gandhi who knitted a lacy shawl and sent it to London with his greetings. The simple gift did not, however, meet with Queen Mary's approval when she first toured the exhibition which was opened to the public after the wedding. The item having been likened to a loincloth, it was hurriedly hidden from view by Princess Margaret when her grandmother made a second tour of inspection a few days later.

In the meantime, royal guests, representing nearly all the past and present European royal dynasties, arrived in London over the weekend 15–17 November 1947 and the King and Queen in their off-duty moments spent most of their time darting from one station to the next to greet them. There hadn't been a congregation of

LEFT: An unusual view of the bride's magnificent train as she and the Duke of Edinburgh leave Westminster Abbey.

RIGHT: Princess Elizabeth, Duchess of Edinburgh, and her bridegroom after the ceremony.

royalty on such a scale in England since the days of Queen Victoria. Queen Mary noted in her diary, following the pre-wedding ball at Buckingham Palace, that she had met many old friends and, just as noteworthy considering her age, that she had stood for almost three hours!

Among the old friends the Queen Mother referred to were King Frederick and Queen Ingrid of Denmark, King Peter and Queen Alexandra of Yugoslavia, the Kings of Romania and Norway, Queen Frederika of Greece, the Princess Regent of the Netherlands and Prince Bernhard, Queen Victoria-Eugenie of Spain, the Duchess of Aosta, the Crown Prince and Princess of Sweden, and King Leopold III's brother, the Regent Prince Charles of the Belgians, with whom Princess Elizabeth's name had once been linked. Notable absentees were the bridegroom's German relations, and in particular his sisters, Theodora and Margarita, who had married princes of Baden and Hohenlohe-Langenburg respectively; omissions that were not difficult to justify given the prevailing climate of opinion.

The day of the wedding itself – 20 November – was ushered in by rain and a cold wind. But the elements failed to dampen the high spirits of all those who flocked to London in their tens of thousands in the hope of catching a glimpse of the royal bride. In the Mall they stood up to eighteen-deep; Trafalgar Square, Whitehall and Northumberland Avenue were packed to capacity, and good-natured policemen waved the more enterprising down from lamp-posts and statues. How different it was from the wedding of Queen Victoria and Prince Albert a century before, when onlookers shinned up trees, clinging to branches until they broke, showering bodies on to those below, and when standing-room only, on a sturdy kitchen table, could be had for one shilling per head.

In her bedroom at the palace Princess Elizabeth (according to her governess, Marion Crawford, who 'revealed all' in her book *The Little Princesses*, much to the chagrin of the Royal Family) had to keep pinching herself in order to believe that it was really happening. Miss Crawford's 'little Princess' was about to become the Duchess of Edinburgh. The previous evening Lieutenant Mountbatten had officially become a fully fledged member of the British Royal House when the King, having already bestowed on Philip the Most Noble Order of the Garter, created him Duke of Edinburgh, Baron Greenwich and Earl of Merioneth – completed by the rank and style of 'Royal Highness'. So far as the already printed wedding ceremonial was concerned, however, it wasn't as a duke, or for that matter as a baron or an earl, that the bridegroom entered Westminster Abbey, but simply as Lieutenant Philip Mountbatten, RN. At the end of the service though, with his bride beside him, it was as a Duke that the crowds acclaimed him.

For an hour and more before the ceremony was due to begin, Westminster Abbey gradually became crowded with guests from almost every walk of life. In all, nearly three thousand invitations had been extended and gladly accepted. The choir took its place in the organ loft spanning the nave, the trumpeters appeared in a recess high above the altar from where they were to sound welcoming fanfares upon the arrival of the Queen and her guests and, later, the bride and her father, and the

The wedding group. From left to right, back row: the Hon. Margaret Elphinstone, Lady
Pamela Mountbatten, Lady Mary Cambridge, Princess Alexandra of Kent, Princess Margaret, Lady
Carolyn Montagu-Douglas-Scott, Lady Elizabeth Lambart, Miss Diana Bowes-Lyon. Front row:
Queen Mary, Princess Andrew of Greece, Prince William of Gloucester, Prince Michael of Kent, King
George VI, Queen Elizabeth and the Dowager Marchioness of Milford Haven. With the bride and the
bridegroom is the best man, the Marquess of Milford Haven.

officiating clergy, all gathered in their ecclesiastical robes inside the great west door of the Abbey.

The right atmosphere was set by the choice of pre-wedding music, played on the organ by the Poet Laureate's 'musical' counterpart, the Master of the King's Musick. There was Elgar's '*Sonata in G Major*, Bach's *Fugue in G* and *Jesu, Joy of Man's Desiring*, followed by a selection from Handel's *Water Music*, and finally, Parry's *Bridal March*.

A little before eleven o'clock the bridegroom arrived in naval uniform, wearing his newly acquired Garter Star together with the Star of the Order of the Redeemer – the only visible reminder that he was once a Greek prince. With him was his best man, more properly known in royal circles as the 'groomsman', in the form of a similarly attired Marquess of Milford Haven, Philip's cousin David Mountbatten.

As the colourful tapestry began to take shape, the trumpeters sounded a fanfare to herald the arrival of the Queen and her royal guests. Queen Elizabeth walked slowly beside the stately figure of her mother-in-law, Queen Mary, who had driven to the abbey in her Daimler state car, and had delighted the waiting crowds by becoming the first member of the Royal Family ever to use an interior light so that she might be seen more clearly in the weak daylight. The two Queens nodded and smiled to the congregation as they passed along the nave towards their chairs in the sacrarium.

Moments later, the expectant hush was heightened by the arrival of Princess Elizabeth's attendants – eight bridesmaids, headed by her seventeen-year-old sister, Margaret, and eleven-year-old cousin, Alexandra of Kent; and two small page-boys, the five-year-old Princes Michael of Kent and William of Gloucester, each of whom sported a kilt in the royal tartan. The Hartnell designs for the bridesmaids' dresses had been inspired by various works of art in the Royal Collection, and the finished articles were confections of spangled white tulle with fichu tops, complemented by long white gloves, floral head-dresses and trailing bouquets.

At 11.16 a.m., precisely on time, the bride set out from Buckingham Palace in the splendid maroon and gold Irish State Coach with the King seated beside her. The Princess looked calm now though only a short time before she had had good reason for concern: the band of her tiara had snapped moments before it was to be secured to her veil, something which called for the immediate attention of a hurriedly summoned jeweller. Just as urgent was the hunt for her bouquet which had apparently disappeared in all the excitement. It was eventually located in a refrigerator where a thoughtful footman had placed it to keep the blooms fresh.

Although the press had foreseen an 'austerity wedding', the procession that wound its way to Westminster Abbey encompassed all the traditional splendour of a full-scale royal procession, and the sight overwhelmed the cheering onlookers to whom the war, on that day especially, seemed a thing of the past. There was an added bonus for the crowds too, for instead of a khaki-clad Household Cavalry as had been originally envisaged, they watched 126 troopers of the Sovereign's Escort ride by dressed in full ceremonial uniform, by special command of the King. It was the first

King George VI and Queen Elizabeth stand for a moment in the forecourt of Buckingham Palace after waving farewell to Princess Elizabeth and the Duke of Edinburgh at the start of their honeymoon.

BELOW: A display cabinet showing some of the wedding presents on show at St James's Palace. Prominent among them are the engraved crystal plates, the gift of the American Ambassador.

time that the scarlet tunics and the highly polished helmets and breastplates had been seen at a state occasion for almost a decade; and at Wellington Barracks, the young troopers rehearsed over and over again the art of riding straight-backed while not allowing their helmets to slip over their foreheads as they tended to do.

Then, as the Princess and her father walked beneath the specially erected awning at Westminster, the ancient abbey was suddenly filled with the sound of a bright flourish of trumpets and the distant sound of pealing bells. The brief scene that followed put one in mind of the dance of the cygnets from *Swan Lake*, as the bridesmaids, in their fluffy dresses, surrounded the bride; first arranging her ivory tulle veil secured by her mother's diamond tiara, then straightening her long shimmering train.

Men and women alike watched as if spellbound, for Princess Elizabeth had never looked lovelier. Norman Hartnell had created something of a masterpiece. Scattered over the ivory satin gown – inspired this time by the figures of Botticelli – were garlands of York roses entwined with stars, ears of corn and orange blossom all picked out in raised pearls and crystal, and the pattern was cleverly repeated in satin on the long silk tulle Court train that fell from her shoulders and was carefully carried by the two small princes who attended her.

As the last notes of the fanfare faded away, the voices of the choir blended with the organ in the processional hymn 'Praise my soul the king of heaven', during the singing of which the King led Princess Elizabeth along the nave to the steps of the sacrarium and the vast congregation rose to greet them.

It had been Princess Elizabeth's choice that the actual solemnization of the marriage be taken from the Book of Common Prayer, including the vow to 'obey', and, as a compliment to her parents, that the rest of the service should follow the lines observed at their own marriage in the abbey, almost twenty-five years earlier.

During the first part of the hour-long ceremony, King George remained by his daughter's side as the Dean of Westminster reminded the bridal couple that marriage, 'is not by any to be enterprised, nor taken in hand unadvisedly, lightly, or wantonly ... duly considering the causes for which Matrimony was ordained....' Then it was the turn of Dr Fisher, the Archbishop of Canterbury, who stepped forward to marry the couple simply as Elizabeth Alexandra Mary Windsor and Philip Mountbatten. The simplicity was underlined in the Archbishop of York's address which followed, in which he said: 'Notwithstanding the splendour and national significance of the service ... it is the same as it would be for any cottager who might be married this afternoon in some small country church.'

After the prayers, the Bible reading and the hymns, the Duke and Duchess of Edinburgh crossed the sacrarium and entered the Chapel of Edward the Confessor where, using a solid gold quill pen received as a wedding present from the Chartered Institute of Secretaries (representing the contributions of 18,000 secretaries) they signed the four registers. The King and Queen added their signatures, as did Queen Mary and Philip's mother, Princess Andrew, and then it was time to return to Buckingham Palace for the family photographs and the wedding-breakfast. The royal party returned to their seats, a final fanfare was sounded, and Princess Elizabeth and her husband left Westminster Abbey to the triumphant sound of Mendelssohn's *Wedding March*, a celebrated piece which had been given its inaugural performance at the wedding of Queen Victoria's daughter, the Princess Royal, to Crown Prince Frederick William of Prussia, eighty-nine years earlier.

As the bride and bridegroom stepped into the Glass Coach, the vast crowd opposite the abbey greeted them with a huge roar of approval, almost drowning the bells that pealed in celebration, and the couple received the same reception all the way back to Buckingham Palace from the thousands who had followed the wedding itself on their wirelesses. Later that day, Elizabeth and Philip, accompanied by several hot-water bottles and a corgi or two, rode from the palace in the State landau to the railway station, bound for the first part of their honeymoon at Broadlands in Hampshire, the home of Earl and Countess Mountbatten.

For King George VI, the marriage of his heir had been a particularly poignant occasion, and that evening, in a moment of quiet reflection, he sat down at his desk and wrote to his daughter who was, so soon, to become Queen Elizabeth II. The King wrote:

I was so proud of you and thrilled at having you so close to me on our long walk in Westminster Abbey, but when I handed your hand to the Archbishop, I felt I had lost something very precious. You were so calm and composed during the Service and said your words with such conviction, that I knew everything was all right.

6

The Princess and the Photographer

From the moment Princess Elizabeth became Duchess of Edinburgh, the press levelled its sights on her younger sister Margaret, and began its relentless speculation about which of her many friends, escorts, distant relations and acquaintances would ultimately become her husband.

Few, however, could have envisaged what was shortly to unfold, though in June 1949, as the Princess neared her nineteenth birthday, 'Chips' Channon noted prophetically 'there is already a Marie-Antoinette aroma about her....'

Wildly premature wedding-bells were, nonetheless, already being faintly heard among Fleet Street's gossip-mongers, and speculation was especially active in the early 1950s as observers watched the birth of the so-called 'Margaret Set'. With a little bit of invention the group's days and nights of merry-making were chronicled. As was predictable the limelight was inclined to silhouette the exclusive clique's male members. There was the Earl of Dalkeith, Billy Wallace, Colin Tennant, Simon Phipps (later to become Bishop of Lincoln), the Marquess of Blandford and Mark Bonham-Carter. The list seemed endless and the press had a field day adding more eligible young men to the long line of possibles. The 'set' moved from night club to night club while Margaret became the 'bright young thing' of the 1950s social whirl. She was the first princess to smoke in public, although most newspapers were inclined to paint out the smouldering French cigarette in its long black holder.

Superficially, Princess Margaret was having a whale of a time. But, by now, her feelings for her father's equerry, Group-Captain Peter Townsend, had already begun to simmer, and when her emotion turned into love, courtiers smiled. They called it harmless 'hero worship'; but nobody pointed out the pitfalls of a love which simply could not be. King George reputedly had said that he would have liked 'a boy like Townsend' and the Group-Captain, one of the younger royal aides, got on extremely well with all members of the Royal Family. But for his marital status there really could have been no objection to Princess Margaret seeking him publicly for her husband. As it was Townsend, raised to the post of Deputy Master of the Royal Household in 1950, had spoken about his marital difficulties to the King, who listened with a suitably sympathetic ear, advising him to go through with his divorce from his wife Rosemary with as little fuss as possible.

But at that time, George VI could have had little idea what Peter Townsend's divorce would cost his younger daughter, and certainly few, if any, were aware of a situation soon to reach its head. At this time their eyes and ears were focused upon the King, whose health had begun to fail over the past few years, giving rise to real concern.

In the summer of 1951, Princess Margaret celebrated her twenty-first birthday and officially came of age. As far as the Royal Marriages Act instituted so long ago by George III was concerned, she wasn't free to marry without the sovereign's consent until she was twenty-five, and even then, as a matter of courtesy, the sovereign was usually consulted.

All notions of a possible marriage to Peter Townsend – or anybody else for that matter – together with her frivolous nocturnal gaddings about with her 'set', were smashed to smithereens six months later with the death of the King, who, just six weeks previously, had celebrated his fifty-sixth birthday.

To Princess Margaret, the premature loss of the father she adored was the cruellest blow in her young life. Elizabeth, as Queen, had assumed a rôle in society which even mourning could not allow her to neglect. But Princess Margaret's somewhat unique position within the framework of the modern monarchy would never change. There had, of course, been other royal sisters in history, Mary and Elizabeth Tudor and Mary and Anne Stuart, for example, but then, all four were destined to become queens of England – Margaret was not. Constitutionally speaking, she was always to remain ambiguous.

By the end of 1952, the round of public and private engagements had been resumed, and the Group-Captain (appointed an equerry to the new sovereign) was technically a bachelor again. His divorce had been heard the previous December. As yet, the public knew little or nothing about Princess Margaret's feelings for him, but during the first few months of 1953, various rumours aroused the public's interest. The bond between Princess Margaret and Townsend had grown steadily as each gave the other much needed comfort and support. Princess Margaret was to take a long time to recover from her father's death and Peter's divorce had been far from a jolly affair. But when both realized they were in love, the next step required very careful handling. Certainly Peter was now free to marry again and nobody could accuse Margaret of having come between a man and his wife. Even so, the fact remained that Townsend was now a divorcee and in the 1950s a divorcee simply couldn't consider marriage with a princess of the blood, especially when the Princess's sister was titular head of the Church of England. The Church, then as now, didn't take kindly to a divorce court judge putting 'asunder' what, in their eyes, God had joined together. Twenty years later, the Church's doctrine on divorce, so far as Princess Margaret's situation was concerned, went up in smoke.

In the meantime, however, the pomp and splendour of the coronation of Queen Elizabeth II occupied everybody's thoughts, though on coronation day itself, 2 June 1953, one small action on Princess Margaret's part was to tell the world of her feelings for Peter Townsend. After the lengthy ceremony, an ebullient Princess stepped forward and, while chatting to Townsend, brushed from his tunic a small fleck of thread

– some have since called it an imaginary fleck – and although it was an innocent enough gesture, the fuse had finally been lit and the Margaret–Townsend saga had begun.

No sooner had the news been publicized than the Buckingham Palace hierarchy were to be found dusting down the royal history books. This may have been the second half of the twentieth century, but whether the country would stomach what some may have seen as an up-dated version of the antics of Queen Victoria's 'wicked uncles' was debatable, especially at this stage. Furthermore, the abdication still lingered in many people's minds and a sequel could be lethal in coronation year. The royal advisers decided that Princess Margaret would be best employed – at least for a short time – on an overseas visit while Townsend was hastily found another job; this time far removed from the Royal Family and preferably abroad.

At the time, fortunately or unfortunately, there were one or two overseas postings which needed filling. One of them was the office of air attaché in Brussels; Townsend agreed to go. But there was one added proviso. The position *had* to be filled whilst the Princess was away on an official visit to Bulawayo with her mother, and not one hint of Townsend's transfer was to reach her ears *before* her return from Southern Rhodesia. Townsend bade farewell to his Princess and her mother at Heathrow Airport when they set out on their tour, and shortly afterwards the Group-Captain himself was gone.

Princess Margaret's reaction upon her return – although there have already been one or two versions – can only be imagined; but it was a sad, if not ridiculous, situation hampered by the obstinacy of the Royal household, the government and, of course, the Church. Not one member of these three august bodies faltered in their judgement. A marriage would *not* be allowed.

Chapter and verse of the Royal Marriages Act was thrown at Princess Margaret, as were several sermons delivered by preachers, all too ready to remind her that 'Christian duty is not always pleasant or easy'. But these carefully contrived sermons were aimed at the converted. Margaret already knew all about 'Christian duty'. By the beginning of 1955 matters were about to reach a head. The Princess was packed off on yet another tour of duty, this time to the Caribbean; while at home Winston Churchill was about to hand over the office of prime minister to Anthony Eden, who, ironically, was a divorced man himself. Would *he* have more sympathy for Princess Margaret's cause? In due course, Her Royal Highness would raise the matter of Eden's divorce and wait for a reaction. In the end, this method of approach proved fruitless. Eden represented the views not only of the entire Cabinet, but those of Commonwealth leaders and, as might have been expected, the idea of a Margaret–Townsend marriage continued to be officially vetoed.

It was becoming more and more apparent by this time that the love the couple shared was doomed. Ninety-six per cent of the nation might have been right behind them but the collective voice of the people wasn't powerful enough to sway Court, Cabinet *and* Church, all of whom remained as impassive as ever.

'All I want is to see Peter happy again,' said Townsend's mother, Gladys; and the Duchess of Windsor, who had trodden on the toes of the establishment herself, tactfully told a New York journal, 'I certainly wish her great happiness if she marries him.'

The charitable sentiments continued to flow, even within Parliament and certain sections of the religious community. Willie Hamilton, socialist MP for West Fife, and better known for his scathing criticism of the monarchy, said, 'The Church of England is the opposition to the marriage. . . . They are trying to tell her whom she should marry. It is fantastic.' The *British Weekly*, a Christian inter-denominational journal, stated, 'Free Church and Church of Scotland people believe that Canterbury's views on this matter are mistaken if not so lacking in compassion as to be un-Christian.' So there it was. Townsend himself broke the *impasse* with a decision that it was time to call it a day, and reluctantly Princess Margaret agreed. *They* would never allow a marriage despite their veiled promises and finally, on 31 October 1955, came the now famous statement which Princess Margaret had insisted she make on her own terms. If she had to concede defeat then it would be she, and nobody else, who would have the final word. Her Royal Highness's communiqué read:

I would like it to be known that I have decided not to marry Group-Captain Peter Townsend. I have been aware that, subject to my renouncing my rights of succession, it might have been possible for me to contract a civil marriage. But mindful of the church's teachings that Christian marriage is indissoluble, and conscious of my duty to the Commonwealth, I have resolved to put these considerations before any others.

I have reached this decision entirely alone, and in doing so I have been strengthened by the unfailing support and devotion of Group-Captain Townsend. . . .

During the weeks that followed the announcement the Princess, who had become the 'princess charming' of the more sycophantic women's journals, found herself riding the crest of an enormous wave of deep public sympathy. On 1 November, the 'William Hickey' page of the *Daily Express* suitably summed up the whole episode as follows, even offering a word of caution and advice to the country:

You will be telling the story of Princess Margaret and Peter Townsend not just this year, not just next year. You will tell it to your children as they grow up. You will, some of you, tell it to grandchildren when the new century comes in.

And when you tell it . . . tell it with compassion; tell it with love. For this is one of the great romances of history; a tale of a beautiful Princess and a brave airman who fell in love – and whose love was star-crossed.

It is the story of a medieval tapestry that has come to life in an age of H-bombs and electronics. It was a classic love story; yet the scene was not some walled city not far from 'the wine dark seas' of Homer's Greece; it was not in Verona when Montagues and Capulets strove for power. . . . It was in London; post-war London. In those post-war years when meat was short, and butter and sugar. And when returning servicemen talked in their jargon, and looked tired beyond their years.

And one of these men was Group-Captain Peter Townsend. . . .

Within the next two years, Townsend's eventual successor had established himself on the horizon; young society photographer, Antony Armstrong-Jones.

81

The Princess and the Photographer

Whether or not Princess Margaret had taken much notice of him when she attended the wedding of her old friend Colin Tennant to one of her future ladies-in-waiting, Lady Anne Coke, is not known. But Tony had landed the job of official photographer at the wedding via Elizabeth Cavendish, daughter of the Duke of Devonshire. As a friend and current lady-in-waiting to the Princess, she was to become instrumental in getting HRH and Armstrong-Jones together, in the coming months. Though he may never have headed the list of eligible suitors in the strictest sense, this enterprising young man wasn't exactly without connections – and the world in which he moved was well versed in the intricacies of royal etiquette. His mother was the Countess of Rosse; his uncle, the brilliant designer and interior decorator, Oliver Messel; and his father, Ronald Armstrong-Jones, was a QC. All the same, a little bit of help in gaining access to the unique world of kings and princes didn't come amiss.

At this point Armstrong-Jones, who lived in a flat beneath the Sunlight laundry in Pimlico Road, was to photography what David Hockney was soon to become to the art world, and anybody who was anybody wanted to know him. Tony, who had already been introduced to Princess Marina's eldest son, the present Duke of Kent, and had taken his official twenty-first birthday photographs in 1956, had trained under the Court photographer, Baron. Upon his death his friend, the Duke of Edinburgh, had introduced Armstrong-Jones's work to the Queen. Her Majesty was impressed and commissioned him to take a series of photographs of her two eldest children.

Princess Margaret's subsequent curiosity as to the identity of this young man, was to be satisfied upon her return from yet another overseas tour – this time to East Africa. Lady Elizabeth Cavendish, obviously happy about her new role as Cupid to her royal mistress, introduced them at a dinner party which she gave at her home in Chelsea.

At exactly what point the romance between the Princess and the photographer sprang up isn't altogether clear, but it is fairly safe to say that, after the initial meeting, their relationship went from strength to strength. Tony was lively, well connected in the world of the arts, and in short, he was fun! Up to this point, Princess Margaret's friends of both sexes had all fallen very neatly and predictably into one category – the top drawer. Outsiders didn't really have a chance to get to know her. But all that would change through her relationship with Tony Armstrong-Jones. It was he who was to act as a kind of bridge over which Margaret could cross into the more intimate worlds of the theatre and the arts and, to a certain extent, into the sphere of everyday people.

Quietly, Princess Margaret and Lady Elizabeth would slip away from the restricting environment of royal palaces to an ordinary-looking house on the river, 59 Rotherhithe Street, SE16, in the heart of London's dockland. Here was to be found the now famous 'white room' with its upright piano and empty bird-cage which Tony rented from Bill Glenton, a writer friend. It was to be the scene of many a happy evening.

Intensely beautiful as a young woman, Princess Margaret made a stunning bride. She is seen here on the balcony of the Green Drawing Room at Buckingham Palace on her wedding-day, 6 May 1960.

The Queen and her mother were a little wary and warned Margaret about the possibilities of another 'scandal' as everybody now dubbed the Townsend romance. Margaret, for her part, bit her thumb at the establishment and went on her way.

In 1959, as their relationship began to gather momentum, Tony's twenty-ninth birthday photographs of Princess Margaret were released, and perhaps to the perceptive, they revealed a new serenity. So began what can only be described now as the Snowdons' 'collision course'.

Friends, including Tony's father (himself thrice-married), were already against the idea of a marriage between the couple. But regardless of such opposition and the 'Job's comforters' they encountered among their own circle, an announcement was released from Clarence House on 26 February 1960 that astounded the world. It read:

> It is with the greatest pleasure that Queen Elizabeth the Queen Mother announces the betrothal of her beloved daughter the Princess Margaret to Mr Antony Charles Robert Armstrong-Jones, son of Mr R.O.L. Armstrong-Jones, QC and the Countess of Rosse to which union The Queen has gladly given her consent.

Margaret's reasons behind the engagement must now remain purely speculative. But it is certain that Peter Townsend's engagement, to a young Belgian heiress, Marie-Luce Jamagne, in October 1959, influenced her decision. Indeed, sixteen years after her own marriage (and only two years before her divorce added another chapter to the history of royal marriages), Princess Margaret is said to have admitted that her engagement to Tony, only four months later, was 'no coincidence'.

All the same, despite rumour and counter-rumour, the delighted peoples of the world sent renewed good wishes for the Princess's happiness, when it was announced that the wedding would take place on the morning of Friday 6 May, at Westminster Abbey.

As the wedding-day approached, London assumed a new appearance. Indeed, the streets hadn't looked quite so festive since the coronation. The Mall was bedecked and garlanded. From blue and white flag-poles fluttered white silk banners bearing Tudor roses embossed with the bridal couple's entwined initials (which were sold later for £45 each), and baskets of flowers hung from every lamp-post. The Department of the Environment's *pièce de résistance* was, undoubtedly, a sixty-foot arch of roses suspended from triple-crowned poles, that spanned the Mall at the junction of Stable Yard Road, the entrance to Clarence House where the bride lived with her mother. Other tourist spots, such as Parliament Square, sprouted giant floral maypoles, and shops were decorated with photographs of the Princess and her fiancé.

The Queen declared the day of her sister's wedding a bank holiday for schoolchildren, but it was the adults who snapped up the tickets of admission – some costing as much as £25 each – to the specially erected stands along the route. Thousands more arrived in the capital during the week of the wedding, to stake temporary claim to a few feet of London's pavement – which was, at least, free of charge, and there they intended to stay until the princely pantomime was all over.

Princess Margaret and her bridegroom honour the Queen after the wedding ceremony.

Several times the Princess, who had chosen all the music for the ceremony herself, visited the Dean of Westminster to discuss final details. After a glass of sherry one afternoon, she and Armstrong-Jones were conducted along the nave, to see carpenters at work building the necessary stands for the press, and for the many television cameras that were to be installed. How different from the 1920s, when the bride's parents had been married there. Then it had been considered too irreverent even to *broadcast* the wedding, and here was Princess Margaret, watching cameras being erected actually inside the abbey, waiting to transmit her wedding half-way around the world; zoom lenses, costing £2,000 each, were being employed for the very first time to take close-up images of the bride into millions of homes.

Norman Hartnell, that doyen of royal *haute couture*, received his brief to design the bride's gown and those of her mother and sister. Jeremy Fry, a long-standing friend of the groom's, was chosen as best man, only to be replaced later by Dr Roger Gilliatt, for reasons best known to those privy to such changes of mind. Princess Margaret chose her eight small bridesmaids from among the families of friends and relations. Princess Anne, barely ten years old, would act as chief bridesmaid, and the retinue would be completed by Marilyn Wills, the bride's goddaughter, Angela Nevill, Virginia Fitzroy, Sarah Lowther, Annabel Rhodes, Rose Nevill and Tony's niece, Catherine Vesey.

Invitations were extended to friends, including such stage personalities as Joyce Grenfell and Margaret Leighton; to acquaintances and representatives of the many charitable organizations, such as Barnardo's and the Dockland Settlement, in which the Princess took an active interest; and of course, invitations were extended to various royal families abroad. None of the latter were accepted, with the one exception of the bride's godmother, Queen Ingrid of Denmark, and a handful of German princelings, whose thrones and domains now belong to history.

There was one final rehearsal at the abbey for the Princess and her fiancé the day before the wedding. The Royal Yacht *Britannia*, loaned by the Queen, was moored in the Pool of London in readiness to take the couple out to their honeymoon in the West Indies and, apart from the last-minute details and worries encountered with any wedding, everything was ready. Even so, 'scurrilous rumours' (as one guest put it) persisted, and while certain sections of high society continued to hold their breath the mixed undercurrent of truth and rumour failed to reach the ears of the public at large.

In any event, the Glass Coach, with its splendid Captain's Escort of the Household Cavalry, swung out of the gates of Clarence House the following morning on time and the platitudes began to flow as freely and as predictably as the champagne at the wedding-breakfast.

Friday 6 May 1960 had dawned the most beautiful of early summer days and by noon the morning heat-haze had given way to a temperature of 72°F. Guardsmen, lining the processional route, sweltered in their high-necked tunics, their heads expanding uncomfortably beneath the bamboo frames of their torturous bearskins, and the St John Ambulance Brigade, on Parade as always at such occasions,

ABOVE: Bride, bridegroom and bridesmaids appear on the palace balcony. In the doorway, Queen Elizabeth the Queen Mother.

The royal barge ferries Princess Margaret and her husband out to *Britannia*.

attended to literally thousands of fainting cases throughout the day. For the ingenious not able to find first, second, third . . . sixth or seventh line places, homemade periscopes were hoisted, while others stood on boxes and folding chairs in an attempt to get a glimpse of the royal bride as she passed by with her brother-in-law seated beside her. Londoners rubbed shoulders with people from the West Country, the Midlands and the North, and many a foreign visitor got enthusiastically caught up in the general euphoria of what was, arguably, the most breathtaking royal wedding for many a year.

By the time the appointed hour for the wedding had arrived, not one seat in the abbey stood empty. The bridegroom and Dr Gilliatt had taken their places, so too had such public figures as Sir Winston Churchill, Sir Anthony Eden, Earl Attlee and members of both Houses of Parliament. The bridegroom's family were seated on the north side of the Persian-carpeted sacrarium; the Countess of Rosse in her grey and white brocade outfit, being voted the best-dressed woman in the church – next to the bride herself. Adding to the ever-growing panoply of colour, two banks of flowers, each nine feet tall, composed of lilies, irises, tulips, gladioli, white roses and marguerites, stood sentinel on either side of the high altar.

A fanfare of trumpets greeted the arrival of Her Majesty the Queen, who looked uncharacteristically morose throughout the service. In a full-skirted dress of turquoise silk and lace, she was accompanied by Queen Elizabeth the Queen Mother, in soft gold lamé with a matching hat of swirling ospreys. Princess Marina, elegant as ever, in a sheath dress of yellow organdie sprinkled with sequins, preceded their Majesties, together with her daughter Princess Alexandra, who, on such a hot day, had wisely chosen a long cool-looking dress of aqua-marine slipper satin. The rest of the royal ladies followed suit in outfits of blues; the Princess Royal's cloth-of-gold dress looked somewhat dated, almost as if it had been the dress she had planned to wear at the Queen's wedding thirteen years before when illness suddenly prevented her from attending.

The visiting prelates, in all the glory of their historic copes and stoles, preceded the Archbishop of Canterbury, Dr Fisher – performing his last royal wedding before retiring from office – in his cope and mitre of cream and gold, into the sacrarium. For over half an hour the stately had made their entrances and now everybody awaited the bride.

Inside the great west door stood the bevy of bridesmaids. Hartnell had dressed them, at Princess Margaret's wish, in replicas of her first ballgown, a favourite of her late father. Of white organza, trimmed with lace, each dress was faithfully copied down to the 'Peter Pan' collars and puffed sleeves threaded with blue satin ribbon. Their half-moon head-dresses of fluffy white swansdown only served to enhance their youthfulness.

Finally, the bride arrived. The moment she stepped down from the Glass Coach, the twelve trumpeters raised their silver trumpets and, as she slowly approached the west door looking extremely nervous despite Prince Philip's obvious efforts to calm her, sounded a welcoming flourish. The Dean of Westminster greeted her and for a moment, seemingly miles away, she stood with the Duke, staring straight ahead.

As the great organ began the processional hymn, 'Christ is made the sure foundation', the ivory cross of Westminster moved off along the blue-carpeted nave, and moments later was followed by the Princess and her attendants. A ripple of curtsies and bowing heads ran through the congregation as she passed, and the discreetly positioned television cameras followed her progress under the ornate organ screen, through the choir stalls to the steps of the altar.

For the fashion correspondents, Princess Margaret's wedding-gown was a delight. It had been made from thirty yards of the finest white silk organza, and a fitted V-necked bodice flared out into a full skirt cut into twelve panels, which in turn formed a softly flowing train, several feet long. On her head, clasping a hair-piece curled into a chignon, the magnificent Poltimore diamond tiara (specially acquired for the Princess) was alive with diamond-fire. From it cascaded a long, full veil of white silk tulle, bound with organza, which had been made by St Cyr of Paris. When the bride reached the steps of the sacrarium, she turned and handed her bouquet of orchids and stephanotis to Princess Anne.

The Archbishop of Canterbury asked the bridegroom, 'Antony Charles Robert, wilt thou have this woman to thy wedded wife . . .' and his response in the affirmative was clearly heard. Then, turning now to the Princess, he asked, 'Margaret Rose, wilt thou have this man to thy wedded husband, to live together after God's ordinance in the holy estate of matrimony. . . .' The Princess replied, in her high, clear voice, 'I will.'

As the couple knelt at their scarlet brocade prayer desks, the vows were exchanged, and the bride faltered only once . . . over the phrase 'for better, for worse'. As the plain gold wedding-ring was placed on to the prayer book, the Archbishop of Canterbury raised his hand in blessing: 'In thy Name, O Lord, we hallow and dedicate this ring, that by thy blessing he who gives it and she who wears it . . . may abide together in thy peace. . . .'

The Dean of Westminster read an extract from the Beatitudes, the choir sang 'The Lord is my shepherd', to Schubert's setting; there was more music by Gibbons, Byrd and Holst, and the signing of the marriage registers concluded the service. As Princess Margaret and her husband crossed the sacrarium, the bride dropped a deep, graceful curtsy to the Queen and her mother, and as they reached the nave, the small bridesmaids curtsied to the bride before forming up once again in procession to follow the newly married pair out of the abbey to Purcell's *Trumpet Tune and Airs*.

After the wedding-breakfast, the balcony appearances and the commemorative photographic session in the throne room, the final highlight of the day was the departure of Princess Margaret and the future Earl of Snowdon from Buckingham Palace, *en route* to the Pool of London and the *Britannia*. Members of the Royal Family followed the open-topped Rolls-Royce out into the forecourt throwing confetti – Prince Charles was seen holding a basketful – and many in the crowd followed suit. Through the city the couple drove under police escort, Margaret now wearing a sunshine-yellow silk outfit by Victor Stiebel. By the time they boarded the royal barge which ferried them out to the Royal Yacht, they were way behind schedule. The tide was beginning to ebb, much to the concern of the captain, but the crowds of well-wishers had pressed so tightly against the side of the royal car that the police had found it difficult to clear a path. Indeed it was brought to a halt on so many occasions that one enthusiastic observer found time to scratch a heart on the maroon paintwork, and the limousine had to be resprayed upon its return to the royal mews.

Finally, to the sound of blasting car horns and the whoops and whistles of small river craft, the *Britannia* slipped anchor, just in time to catch the tide. The marine band on board played 'O what a beautiful morning', and Princess Margaret and Tony Armstrong-Jones stood on the bridge, waving to those who lined the river banks – not forgetting a special wave in the direction of Tony's friend, Bill Glenton, who leaned from his windows at the back of the ordinary-looking house in Rotherhithe, where it all began.

7

A Wedding at York

Shortly before Princess Margaret's engagement was announced another royal wedding was already in the making. At a Clarence House party given by the Queen Mother in March 1960 to celebrate her younger daughter's betrothal, the Duke of Kent – a tall young man with the unmistakable Hanoverian features of his predecessors – had eyes for only one girl.

At this time, Edward of Kent was a serving soldier with the Royal Scots Greys, a modest unassuming person little used to the pomp and ceremony of full-scale royal occasions. Edward, who had succeeded to the dukedom of Kent in August 1942 at the age of seven, had been the youngest royal duke since Queen Victoria's grandson, Prince Charles Edward, was born Duke of Albany after his father's death in 1884. He was also, up to this point, one of the few royal figures to be educated in the 'new' style away from home. At first he went to Eton, then later to a school in Switzerland before finishing as a cadet at Sandhurst.

At his side that March evening, attractive in both looks and personality, was Katharine Worsley, known simply as Kate, an equally unassuming kindergarten teacher and a stranger to the public at large. For Miss Worsley, 1960 was to prove her last taste of freedom. Little more than a year later she would join the ranks of royalty as the third Duchess of Kent.

To all intents and purposes, Katharine Lucy Mary, the only daughter of Sir William and Lady Worsley of Hovingham Hall, was an ordinary girl brought up against a typically English background of windswept Yorkshire moors and cricket matches. Her father had his own cricket eleven and a foot in the MCC while one of her three elder brothers was an MP. A closer look at Katharine's family tree revealed a few more surprises, not the least being her descent from the country's one and only dictator, the Lord Protector himself, Oliver Cromwell. But if republican sentiments had once run in the family it wasn't to be overlooked that the Worsleys had been titled landowners in the North Riding of Yorkshire since the time of the Normans, and one ancestor, Sir James Worsley, had been Keeper of the Wardrobe to King Henry VIII and had later been elevated to the governorship of the Isle of Wight by that monarch.

Katharine was almost a stereotype English rose, and she was eminently suited for the rôle destiny had earmarked her to play. She is frank, down-to-earth and undeniably charming, as anybody who has ever had the opportunity of chatting with her will bear witness.

She and Prince Edward had first met at a dance given by Sir William and Lady Worsley in 1956 while the Prince was serving at Catterick, and from that time on their future together seemed assured. To the English, despite their reputation for being rather reserved, romance is a thinly veiled but very important characteristic, and Princess Marina's announcement of her son's engagement on 8 March 1961 was well received by the nation at large. Furthermore, the prospect of the couple's wedding, precisely three months later on Thursday 8 June, put many older people in mind of Marina's own marriage. Twenty-seven years later, the Princess, who had been a widow for nearly twenty years by now, was to watch her son – the very image of his father – take his place beside his bride beneath the vast vaulted roof of York Minster, the Westminster Abbey of the North, where, in 1328, King Edward III had married Princess Philippa of Hainault.

For the Duke and Miss Worsley, the public acknowledgement of their engagement was the culmination of the inevitable waiting-game which royalty often find an unavoidable facet of romance. For the six months preceding her engagement, Katharine Worsley lived in Canada with her brother John and his young family. When she returned to England, it was officially as the Duke of Kent's fiancée. On 8 March there was a family lunch at Kensington Palace with Princess Marina and Kate's parents, and the following day the couple drove to Buckingham Palace to lunch with the Queen, who had 'gladly given her consent' to her cousin's engagement.

During the next few weeks, Princess Marina took her future daughter-in-law under her wing, and on the all-important subject of Katharine's wedding-dress the Princess suggested her own principal designer, John Cavanagh. As a youth, he had worked under the man who had made her own wedding-dress, Edward Molyneux. The arrangement worked well. The bride-to-be admired Cavanagh's work and discussed with him the sort of gown she had in mind. The designer lost no time in transferring Miss Worsley's ideas to paper, and within days of their initial meeting had presented two or three thumbnail sketches for her approval.

Once the design had been chosen it was left to Cavanagh to have the material made. And whilst the looms of a small, reliable French company diligently set about weaving 237 yards of shimmering white silk gauze enhanced by an attractive pearlized motif, Cavanagh concentrated on the question of concealing details of the design from the eyes and ears of the press at his elegant Mayfair salon. From his staff of fitters and seamstresses he handpicked a small team, set aside one workroom on the second floor, blacked out its windows and had the existing door reinforced with steel which was to remain locked at all times.

In the meanwhile Princess Marina's office, in conjunction with the Queen's Household, worked feverishly on the arrangements for the wedding at York. The Crown had bowed to the age-old tradition of allowing the bride to be married in her own locality. Despite a heavy week of public engagements, culminating in the ceremony

ABOVE: The marriage ceremony of the Duke of Kent and Miss Worsley on 8 June 1961.

BELOW: Bride and bridegroom, with the best man, Prince Michael, pose for a group photograph with their eleven attendants.

of Trooping the Colour to celebrate her official birthday, the Queen had no qualms about travelling north and spending the night aboard the royal train.

By the end of April, John Cavanagh had set to work on the bridal gown with its small stand-away collar, tight bodice and diaphanous skirt. Indeed, so immense was the satin-edged double train that when Miss Worsley and Princess Marina went along to the first fitting, both exchanged anxious glances and expressed well-reasoned concern. It literally swamped the workroom. Unflustered, Cavanagh managed to persuade them that their worries were unfounded. Naturally, he explained, any train fifteen feet long would appear impractical in the confined space of a comparatively small workroom, but that wasn't to be the setting of the wedding. Katharine and Princess Marina were willing to give Cavanagh the benefit of the doubt, but how would the fabric behave when the bride was required to kneel and stand unaided? With no further ado, the designer produced a stack of telephone directories roughly the height of the faldstool on which Katharine would have to kneel. She practised the movements and all was well. With that small hurdle out of the way, however, another presented itself. The train was found to drag on the carpeted floor, and although the nave at York Minster would not be covered, the sacrarium would be. It was there at the end of the service that the new Duchess of Kent would have to curtsey to the Queen. As things stood at that moment it looked almost impossible for Katharine to effect the movement as gracefully as she wished. Once again, the designer had the perfect solution. As the bride and bridegroom approached Her Majesty, the young Duchess should effect a half-turn in the Queen's direction, step back into the folds of her gown, thus releasing the tension on her train, and with head slightly bowed, perform her act of homage. There and then Mr Cavanagh offered his arm, Miss Worsley linked it with her own, curtsied and another problem had been taken care of.

A few weeks later one other person outside the small group responsible for the gown was let in on the zealously guarded secret of its design. He was the bride's milliner who was to produce her wedding-veil – another sweeping expanse of white tulle. In fact, there were to be three identical veils. One would be worn by Katharine's understudy during the wedding rehearsals, another would be worn by the bride at the ceremony itself and the third would be kept at Hovingham Hall as a standby to be worn for the official Cecil Beaton photographs if need be.

On the day of the wedding the unpredictable English climate was at its most undecided. Heavy rain was broken by bright sunshine only to be marred again by threatening clouds. For nearly an hour the thirteen bells of the Minster's south-west tower pealed non-stop and the ancient building with its vast, gaunt perpendicular architecture came alive with every imaginable colour as the guests took their places. Above all things, this royal wedding was a simple unpretentious occasion. There were few uniforms in evidence, save those of the Queen's Body-Guard of the Honourable Corps of Gentlemen-at-Arms, in scarlet tunics and gold helmets,

The Duchess of Kent tells one of her small bridesmaids to smooth her dress out. On the right is the chief bridesmaid, Princess Anne.

and a handful of the Duke's fellow officers; those who were to sound the welcoming fanfares and those who were to furnish the guard of honour.

Beyond the west door, almost hidden by scaffolding as restoration work was being carried out, the crowds of local people were massed. Unlike a wedding in London, with its ever-expanding cosmopolitan population, this was, in essence, a local event.

As those inside the Minster, many of whom had travelled from London and the south, waited for the processions to begin, a selection of music was played on the great organ. There was Bach's *Prelude and Fugue in G*, Herbert Howells' *Siciliano for a High Ceremony*, and the *Prelude on 'Rhosymedre'* by Ralph Vaughan Williams. Then, shortly after two o'clock, the first procession of the day arrived. Lord Mountbatten with his daughters led Crown Princes Harald and Constantine, heirs to the thrones of Norway and Greece, along the nave, together with Crown Princess Margrethe of Denmark, Princess Irene of the Netherlands, Prince and Princess Alexander of Yugoslavia and Lord and Lady Harewood. A quarter of an hour later, Queen Elizabeth the Queen Mother, dressed in pale blue chiffon and lace, arrived. She was accompanied by Princess Margaret – by now expecting her first baby – dressed in a blue silk duster coat with matching tulle halo hat, Mr Antony Armstrong-Jones and, among other assorted royalties, Queen Victoria-Eugenie of Spain, the daughter of Princess Beatrice, youngest child of Queen Victoria. For her this wedding must have seemed a far cry from her own. On that day in Madrid, now so long ago, extremists wrought havoc as a bomb was hurled at the bridal procession and the young queen had to change her blood-spattered white satin gown before attending the reception.

The Queen Mother paused with her family to chat with fellow guests behind them – Lady Patricia Ramsay, Princess Sophia of Greece and Don Juan Carlos of Spain – before Princess Marina entered the Minster with her daughter Alexandra. The bridegroom's mother on this day of days had chosen an elegant Cavanagh outfit of champagne silk organdie, lavishly embroidered with diamanté and gold and silver thread. To match, she wore a large cartwheel hat of toning osprey feathers. Princess Alexandra had chosen a silk outfit of azalea pink with a toque of the same shade.

Ten minutes later a trumpet fanfare announced the arrival of Her Majesty the Queen, dressed in an outfit of lilac silk with a curiously shaped hat to match. As she made her way along the nave, accompanied by Prince Philip dressed in the uniform of a field-marshal, his ceremonial sword scraping the ground as he walked, the choir sang the National Anthem.

That day, no fewer than forty-six television cameras were located inside York Minster and along the route taken by the Royal Family. As the Queen's procession, headed by the Gentlemen-at-Arms, the residentiary canons, the Dean and the Archbishop of York, reached their places in the wedding 'theatre', the various cameras were marking the arrival of the eleven children who had just driven the twenty-three miles from Hovingham Hall. Headed by Princess Anne there were eight bridesmaids and three page-boys. The girls, dressed in long white organdie 'Kate Greenaway' dresses, carried posies of roses and wore rosebuds in their hair. In fact there were so many roses – white and cream, merging into yellow – that the occasion was dubbed 'the White Rose Wedding of York'.

Then finally, at thirty-three minutes past two, just three minutes late, the bride herself arrived. Contrary to royal custom, Katharine's face was covered by an extra panel of veiling fastened by diamond pins tucked under her head-dress. This cloud-like addition to her full-length veil was designed to be removed easily when the ceremony reached its conclusion.

The trumpeters of the Royal Scots Greys sounded a flourish as Katharine entered the Minster on the arm of her father. Just for a moment as she stood framed by the ancient arch of the great west door, there was something of a medieval flavour about this royal wedding. Or was it no more than a fleeting impression prompted merely by Miss Worsley's appearance: her narrow diamond tiara tilted very slightly forward, and the shafts of light cascading from the great east window (which contains over two thousand square feet of glass, making it the largest medieval stained-glass window in the world) catching the misty fabric of her gown?

The feeling of long ago faded, however, as the organ opened the first hymn of the service, 'O Praise ye the Lord'. The bride's procession began to move slowly down the nave and had Katharine been able to watch herself at that moment, she would have realized that the immensity of her train was indeed, as Cavanagh had predicted, no match for the vastness of York Minster. Behind her, the small attendants wandered untidily, obviously far too overawed by the hundreds of staring faces to worry too much about keeping in line.

At the foot of the altar steps, the Duke of Kent, resplendent in the ceremonial uniform of his regiment with the dark blue sash of the Grand Cross of the Victorian Order across his chest, waited with his brother and best man. Prince Michael, then at Sandhurst, wore the dark ceremonial uniform of an officer cadet – a sharp contrast to his brother's uniform which, incidentally, had not been worn since before the war.

The marriage service itself was based on the 1928 Prayer Book though, to the surprise of many, the vows incorporated a brief section from the 1662 Prayer Book, including the word 'obey', there at the request of the bride. Beyond that the service was simple and true to form. Edward took Katharine to be his lawfully wedded wife, and placed a very simple gold wedding-ring on her finger.

Princess Marina watched her son with some emotion, occasionally dabbing at her eyes with a small white handkerchief and Princess Alexandra turned to her mother now and then to urge her to relax. The choir quietly sang Psalm CXI: 'I will give thanks unto the Lord with my whole heart: secretly among the faithful, and in the congregation: The works of the Lord are great: Sought out of all them that have pleasure therein ...' The Dean of York led those assembled in prayer and shortly afterwards it was time for the Duke and his bride to leave the sacrarium for the choir of the minster where the marriage registers were signed.

Then finally, with all the formalities dealt with, the trumpets sounded a last fanfare and to Widor's magnificent *Toccata in F* the bride and bridegroom returned to the sacrarium to pay homage to the Queen. As they passed the late fifteenth-century organ screen containing eight statues of Plantagenet kings from William the Conqueror to Henry VI, the new Duchess of Kent's veil got caught on the altar steps. To avert disaster she stood perfectly still, beamed at her husband and then, when her veil was freed, continued on her way.

Outside, they passed beneath a ceremonial arch of swords to be greeted by the skirl of a piper, the sound of the Minster's thirteen bells and the acclaim of the crowds lining the route through the city and out along the country lanes to Hovingham. There, on the lawns of the hall, the wedding-reception for family, friends and members of staff was held beneath a vast multicolour-striped marquee.

Later that afternoon the Duke and Duchess of Kent bade farewell to their guests and left York for the quiet seclusion of the Queen Mother's estate, Birkhall, in Scotland, for the first part of their honeymoon. Boarding one of the small bright red Herons of the Queen's Flight at nearby RAF Linton, the newly married couple discovered that a light snack of salmon sandwiches together with three bottles of vintage champagne had been provided with the Queen's compliments. In case they needed something to do during the flight, a pile of evening newspapers had also been taken aboard.

8

The Freedom of Choice

Not since Princess Margaret's surprise engagement in 1960 had the press made so much of a royal event. In 1961 the Duke of Kent had married Katharine Worsley in the quiet setting of York, and although undoubtedly a popular occasion, it failed to generate quite the same amount of interest and enthusiasm that was to envelop Princess Alexandra's wedding two years later.

One of the reasons for this royal wedding's particular success was that Alexandra had given the overall image of the monarchy the kind of boost unknown since Princess Elizabeth came to the throne in 1952 as a 25-year-old. At that time the idea of a young and attractive sovereign was like a coat of fresh paint to Britain's oldest institution. But though Elizabeth II was destined to become one of the most popular monarchs of all time, her natural diffidence and the very nature of her office meant that any informality that might have emerged earlier was suppressed by protocol.

Princess Alexandra, as a junior member of the Royal Family, had an easier task ahead of her. As a result, she not only topped royal popularity polls but injected into the Royal Family's way of life a brand of informality that rapidly became her trademark – earning her not only the affection of the nation at large, but also the respect of many a hardened republican. Indeed, there was nothing contrived about this young woman – once described by Chips Channon as 'a whirlwind of a girl' – and the public, with its knack for spotting self-seeking 'do-gooders', was quick to recognize her individuality.

Much of Alexandra's relaxed approach to her job, as she would be the first to admit, was directly attributable to her mother's influence and to the standards she set during her own life. This is easy to understand when one looks into the Kent family's background. By ordinary standards they were, of course, well-off. By royal standards they were not and, following the death of her husband, in a flying accident over Scotland in the summer of 1942, Princess Marina was definitely considered the poor relation. By that time she not only had three children to bring up – the youngest of them, Michael, was seven weeks old – but a household to run. It was an almost impossible situation, given the fact that there was no vast fortune to be inherited, and Marina's income was little more than her RAF widow's pension. Economy immediately became the keyword in the Princess's life. She gave up her London home and moved permanently to Coppins, the house her husband had inherited from his maiden-aunt, Princess Victoria, daughter of Edward VII, at Iver in Buckinghamshire. Reluctantly, Princess Marina was forced to sell her husband's cherished collection of antiques, followed by several of the more valuable pieces of her own jewellery. From childhood, therefore, Princess Alexandra and her two brothers were to learn that royal privilege – so far as they were concerned – had its limitations. An invitation to attend a charity gala at Covent Garden, all expenses paid, or an overseas tour, by courtesy of Her Majesty's Government, may not have stretched the family's purse-strings to any great extent, but at home everything else had to be paid for.

This enforced modesty, the life of royalty with a small 'r', became a natural characteristic. So far as the monarchy as a whole was concerned, it could have had no finer representative than Princess Alexandra to lead it into the 'swinging sixties', a decade that was to herald many significant changes in the life of both the Royal Family and the nation.

By the time their engagement was announced in 1962, Princess Alexandra had known the Hon. Angus Ogilvy, a city businessman and the second son of the twelfth Earl of Airlie, for about eight years. The betrothal statement, issued from Princess Marina's grace-and-favour residence at Kensington Palace (a home offered by the Queen to her aunt in the 1950s), said that it was 'with the greatest pleasure' that the Dowager Duchess of Kent told the world of her only daughter's impending marriage. It was also with the greatest pleasure that Angus Ogilvy told his friends to listen out for the news bulletins during the afternoon of 29 November because, unknown to the majority of his associates, he was about to join the ranks of the Royal House of Windsor.

That afternoon, the couple came down the steps into the surprisingly small garden at Kensington Palace to pose for the press; Princess Alexandra (not that it wasn't obvious already) telling journalists that she was 'so very, very happy'. Nearby, Princess Marina watched proudly with the Earl and Countess of Airlie, before being summoned before the cameras to form a family group. Historically, the significance of the date seemed to have been lost on most people. Certainly 1934 seemed a long time ago, but on that day in that year, Princess Marina had married Alexandra's father. For Marina, therefore, it was undoubtedly a poignant anniversary; for her daughter, it was the beginning of a whole new chapter.

Born on Christmas Day 1936, Princess Alexandra was now twenty-five. A tall, good-looking young woman with light brown hair and alert hazel eyes, she was as much her mother's daughter as the Duke of Kent was his father's son. As they grew older and the lives of both parents became a memory, the family likeness was to assume an almost uncanny similarity.

The Princess's fiancé on that engagement day came across as a quiet man; had Alexandra's sense of fun led her in the past to bright society parties and fashionable night clubs, one might have thought of Mr Ogilvy as an incongruous choice of bridegroom. Instead, he seemed ideal. Eight years older than the Princess and handsome

With her 21-foot train flowing out behind her, Princess Alexandra enters the abbey on the arm of the Duke of Kent, followed by her seven attendants.

in a rugged sort of way, he held some fifty-six directorships and took an interest in a great many charities. One of them was The Friends of the Elderly & Gentlefolk's Help – the patrons of which were the Queen and her mother, with Princess Margaret as president. But his family's connections with the Royal Family went much deeper than that. Mabell, Countess of Airlie, Angus's grandmother, had been a lady-in-waiting and close friend of Princess Alexandra's grandmother, Queen Mary, for over fifty years; his father had been Lord Chamberlain to Queen Elizabeth the Queen Mother from the time of her coronation in 1937; and much later, his sister-in-law, the American-born Countess of Airlie, was to become an extra lady-in-waiting to the present Queen. Now, Mr Ogilvy was responsible for forging an even deeper and more personal link with the Royal House; a few weeks after the engagement a further statement from Princess Marina's office announced that the wedding of Her Royal Highness Princess Alexandra of Kent to the Hon. Angus Ogilvy would take place at Westminster Abbey at noon, on Wednesday 24 April 1963. It wouldn't be a state occasion along the lines of Princess Margaret's wedding three years before, and there wouldn't be a public holiday. As with the Kents' marriage, the spectacle of carriage processions would be ruled out though the Princess and her bridegroom were invited to drive from the abbey to St James's Palace (where the wedding-breakfast was to be held) in the Glass Coach, escorted by a travelling party of the Household Cavalry.

To transport the bride from her home in Kensington to Westminster, the Queen put at her cousin's disposal her newly built Phantom V Rolls-Royce state car; a gleaming maroon vehicle with a hood that could be removed easily to reveal a clear perspex roof, affording the crowds an uninterrupted view of the bride.

As with the royal wedding in 1961, the designer chosen to make Princess Alexandra's wedding-gown was John Cavanagh, and when he visited the bride-to-be and her mother at Kensington Palace for an informal discussion, he discovered that Alexandra already had firm ideas of the type of dress she wanted. To begin with it had to be lace, following a plain, classic design: no frills and flounces, no bows or unnecessary trimmings. After the meeting Cavanagh took back to his salon two very valuable articles. The first was the antique wedding-veil of Lady Patricia Ramsay who, as Princess Patricia of Connaught, had worn it at her own wedding in Westminster Abbey forty-four years earlier; and the second was a length of old Valenciennes lace, once owned by Alexandra's maternal grandmother, Princess Nicholas of Greece.

Lady Patricia had presented her own bridal veil to her distant cousin because she felt it might be useful. But although it may have seemed a romantic idea that Alexandra should, perhaps, wear a bridal veil with such a long history – it will be recalled that Queen Charlotte was once the veil's owner – it would be impractical for a 1960s bride to wear something quite so outmoded. There were no hurt feelings, however, since the thing Princess Alexandra admired most was the veil's delicate pattern of tiny acorns and oak-leaves. Could the design be reproduced for her own gown? she asked. The answer was no, not in England. So the job, together with Lady Patricia's veil, was entrusted to a small French company who diligently and discreetly wove the fabric while the designer came to an arrangement with the British Customs that when the material finally arrived in England, it need not be declared as eighty yards of finest magnolia-tinted lace for Princess Alexandra's wedding-gown. The reason for the secrecy was plain enough: the press! As it was, Cavanagh's staff had to resist the bribes that were offered for 'inside' information.

As the wedding-day approached any inside information would have revealed a slight change in plan so far as the overall look of the Princess's bridal attire was concerned. The designer had hit upon a novel idea and fortunately it was one that also appealed to Alexandra. The flash of inspiration came one evening as the bride slipped on her gown and stood in front of a full-length mirror. Mr Cavanagh lifted what was to have been a sweeping Court train falling from the Princess's shoulders and suddenly suggested that the train could be worn as the veil – all twenty-one feet of it. It had never been done before! 'I'll show you what I mean,' the designer said enthusiastically, and draped it over the Princess's head. The original idea for a full-length traditional white tulle veil was scrapped and Cavanagh added the wide border of Valenciennes lace to the 'new-look' head-dress.

The finished creation looked superb. The wedding-dress had a high round neck-line edged with appliqué lace sprigs – also to be found trimming the long tight-fitting sleeves and hem – mounted on white tulle and hand embroidered with thousands of gold paillettes which added the merest shimmer as the Princess walked. The slim skirt fell in sculptured folds to form a train some twenty-one feet long. To secure the magnificent veil Princess Alexandra would wear the diamond fringe tiara given as a wedding-present to her mother by the City of London in 1934 and worn at her own wedding to Prince George.

As might have been expected, the task of designing and making the wedding-day outfits for the Queen, the Queen Mother and Princess Margaret fell to Norman Hart-nell; but the bridesmaids' dresses and the outfit to be worn by the bride's mother remained in John Cavanagh's capable hands.

To the world at large, the royal wedding was to be an international event only in-asmuch as it was being screened in several European countries. Commercially one might say it provided light relief to some of the world's more pressing problems.

On 22 April, a host of foreign royal guests descended on Windsor Castle *en masse* and the following day the Court Circular read a little like an international *Who's Who* of reigning and defunct royal houses. The King of Norway, the Queen of Greece, the Queen of Denmark, Queen Victoria-Eugenie of Spain, Queen Helen of Romania, the Crown Prince of Greece, the Crown Prince of Norway, Princess Irene of Greece, Princess Anne-Marie of Denmark, Princess Irene of the Netherlands, Princess Mar-griet of the Netherlands, the Princess Hohenlohe-Langenburg, the Prince and Prin-cess of the Asturias, the Margrave and Margravine of Baden, Prince and Princess George of Hanover, the Duchess of Aosta, the Prince and Princess of Hesse and the Rhine, Prince Ludwig of Baden, Princess Beatrix of Hohenlohe-Langenburg, Prince Ruprecht of Hohenlohe-Langenburg, Prince and Princess Frederick

ABOVE: Her Majesty the Queen kneels as her cousin and the Hon. Angus Ogilvy pray before the high altar of Westminster Abbey.

BELOW: Princess Alexandra, the Hon. Mrs Angus Ogilvy and her husband pose for an official photograph at St James's Palace following their wedding.

The bridal procession passing through the organ screen at the conclusion of the marriage service.

Windisch-Graetz and Princess Clarissa of Hesse, said the Court Circular, 'have arrived at the castle'. That so many had merely 'arrived' really did seem the understatement of the entire wedding festival. But no doubt Queen Victoria would have been beside herself with delight had she been able to see so many of her descendants gathered together under one roof; especially since they were all there to attend the biggest and most lavish ball ever seen at Windsor since the long-distant days of her own reign.

In fact there were as many guests at the ball, held in the massive Waterloo Chamber which was built to commemorate Wellington's victory over Napoleon a century-and-a-half before, as were invited to attend the wedding itself. Two thousand men and women all in their finest clothes drove up to the floodlit castle for the start of the ball at nine. Women with and without titles sported a spectacular array of tiaras and it rather looked as though every couture house in London had been designing, cutting and sewing for months.

The Royal Family all assembled for dinner at seven, which the Queen, wearing a white lace gown sewn with iridescent white beads and crystal, hosted in an adjoining state room. Princess Alexandra, dressed in a long tight-fitting gown of chalk-white silk with a magnificent pearl and diamond tiara set on her upswept hair, drove from Kensington Palace with her mother and fiancé. Only a short time before Angus had smashed into the back of another car outside the Albert Hall with the result that he arrived to meet his bride in a dented Jaguar and with a limp to hinder his dancing.

At nine o'clock, the doors were swung open by a pair of liveried pages to reveal Her Majesty with the Duke of Edinburgh and the bride and bridegroom. Joe Loss's orchestra – commissioned so often before and since to play at such occasions – struck up a Strauss waltz and the Queen signalled to her cousin and Mr Ogilvy to lead the dancing, which they did. Up in the gallery Prince Charles and Princess Anne looked down on the party – the fifteen-year-old prince filming the occasion with a ciné camera and his thirteen-year-old sister telling him to include various guests with familiar faces who swirled past on the dance-floor. Shortly after midnight with the ball in full swing, the orchestra changed from its sedate waltzes and fox-trots to music for the year's 'in' dance – at the time it was the Twist – and to prove to their younger relations that they were not to be considered out of touch, both the Queen and Prince Philip joined in and, by all accounts, did it extremely well.

The suave Mr Noël Coward looked on intently, smoking a cigarette through a particularly long cigarette-holder, and one newsman later wondered whether another Ruritanian musical might not be on the way as a result. Some of the royal gardeners were there too with their watering-cans at the ready, set the task of discreetly reviving wilting plants. The ball lasted all night and as the floodlighting paled with the arrival of dawn, the last guests drove off down the Long Walk. Princess Alexandra had stayed until 3.15 a.m., just a little longer than some of her other royal relations who had to get back home. Princess Margaret and Lord Snowdon, who left shortly after

3 a.m., were cheered by a small crowd who faithfully waited outside the gates of the castle in the hope of catching a glimpse of some of the celebrities.

In the meantime, the wedding gifts for Princess Alexandra and Mr Ogilvy that continued to flood into Kensington Palace were being carefully recorded and, of course, acknowledged. The Durham Light Infantry, of which Princess Alexandra is Colonel-in-Chief, gave a Sheraton mahogany circular library table; the North Irish Horse sent their Honorary Colonel a silver model of a horse set on a walnut plinth; and the Queen's Own Rifles of Canada (of which the Princess was Colonel-in-Chief) presented an inscribed silver bowl. The Wellington West Coast and Taranaki Regiment gave the couple an eighteenth-century walnut grandfather clock; and Princess Marina's own regiment, the Queen's Own Buffs, Royal Kent Regiment gave a breakfast set and table; whilst the Devonshire and Dorset Regiment gave a Chippendale mahogany bureau.

From the government and people of Australia – where Princess Alexandra had been such a huge success during her tours 'down-under' (and where shortly after her marriage they were to ask for Alexandra's permanent presence as Governor-General) – a set of eight candlesticks, cast and hand-chased in Australian silver, were received; there was also a hand-woven Tai Ping carpet from the government of Hong Kong.

The congregation of St Mary Abbots Church in Kensington where the Princess and her family regularly worshipped presented a blue and gold Spode dinner service, and the Kensington Palace domestic staff presented Princess Alexandra with a cashmere car rug embroidered with her own personal cypher – a pair of linked 'A's surmounted by a coronet. (This cypher was first designed for and adopted by an earlier Alexandra – the Princess's great-grandmother who became the queen of Edward VII.) There were also gifts from the several charities which the Princess headed either as president or patron, and it says much in Alexandra's favour that they all took great care in their selection of wedding-presents. Since none of Princess Alexandra's appointments are ever looked upon as purely nominal offices, the appreciation of the Council and staff of the Guide Dogs for the Blind Association, Queen Alexandra's Royal Naval Nursing Service, the Royal Commonwealth Society for the Blind, the Junior Red Cross and the London Association for the Blind was shown when they presented their gifts of four George III pierced silver salt cellars, a silver cigarette box, a rectangular mirror framed with needlework and velvet, a pair of Dutch walnut china cabinets, and two green leather albums with a pair of matching photograph frames. The list seemed endless. Yet even so, every article would be found a place once the Princess and her husband moved into their new home, Thatched House Lodge in Richmond Park.

A mellow two-storey Georgian building, set in four acres of sloping gardens, the house takes its name from the picturesque thatched summer-house which was built in 1772 by Sir Robert Walpole, who often entertained King George III there when the monarch hunted at Richmond. Thatched House, although by no means a grace-

and-favour residence, is still Crown property and consequently Angus Ogilvy was required to take a lease from the Crown lessee.

On the day of the Windsor Ball, the bride and bridegroom drove to Westminster Abbey for their last wedding rehearsal. Crowds who had found their way into Dean's Yard mobbed the couple as they arrived, and one or two children did get knocked over when the adults rushed forward for a glimpse of the Princess. Alexandra looked concerned, but when assured that nobody had been hurt she and Angus disappeared with the Dean of Westminster, Dr Abbott, through the long shadows of the Norman undercroft. Princess Marina was there too that afternoon, and so was Princess Anne who was to act as chief bridesmaid for the third time at a royal wedding.

The final rehearsal, on the day before the wedding itself, was mainly for the children, Simon Hay, the young Master of Ogilvy, Emma Tennant, Georgina Butter, Doune Ogilvy and the beguiling six-year-old Archduchess Elisabeth of Austria, led by Princess Anne. Princess Alexandra's stand-in, Lady Margaret Hay, pinned a long white train to her coat and moved up and down the nave once or twice, whilst it was stressed to the page-boys how important it was *not* to step on the train the Princess would be wearing on the morrow. The rehearsal went off well and one official was heard to say, 'Much smoother than when we rehearsed Margaret's.'

While the children were being put through their paces, the bride and bridegroom were holding a small reception at Kensington Palace for some of the people they had met abroad. At Windsor, however, a party of a different kind was taking place, – in the shape of a royal coach party. If the sight of one or two motor coaches on hire for the day and packed with smiling royalty looked a trifle incongruous, it was still considered the best way of conducting a guided tour through Windsor Great Park and the surrounding area before stopping off at the Hind's Head in Bray for an informal pub lunch. Among those in the first bus was the Queen with the King of Norway beside her, whilst Prince Philip took the 'courier's' seat next to the driver.

That evening, instead of the traditional stag night, Angus gave a dinner party for his parents, his brothers and sisters-in-law, whilst Alexandra spent the evening at home with some friends in a rather more traditional wedding-eve 'hen' night.

Meanwhile, along the route of the procession, people were already beginning to arrive to snap up their places. First claimed were those prized kerb-side spots along the Mall, though in Whitehall notices had been erected which ordered 'No camping here before midnight'. Undeterred, 'campers' crossed the road and held their own party in St James's Park until such time as they could take up their posts for the night.

Princess Alexandra rose early on the morning of her wedding and although she wasn't able to eat her breakfast she appeared the least nervous of all those surrounding her. 'Now let's keep calm,' she reputedly told them, 'and everything will be fine.' Early callers at her home were her hairdresser and his assistants followed by John Cavanagh, who was there to see that all was well with the bridal gown.

Princess Marina and her daughter-in-law, the young Duchess of Kent, slipped upstairs to change and Alexandra's brother Edward, immaculate in morning-dress, hovered in the background. He and the Duchess had returned to London from Hong Kong – where the Duke was stationed with his regiment – in order that he should give the bride away.

By the time the clock above the main archway of this red-brick palace, once described by the diarist John Evelyn as 'a very neat villa', struck eleven o'clock, the bride and her family were ready. Princess Marina's dark-blue Rolls-Royce with its distinctive number-plate YR 11 (YR being a reference to 'York Royal' and the days when Prince George and the future Duke of Windsor shared their first car) drew up outside the white pillared entrance to her home, and behind it the Queen's own car waiting for the bride.

Little more than half-an-hour later the first of the foreign royal guests had arrived at Westminster Abbey. Then came the members of the British Royal Family who were to take up their places in the sacrarium: Princess Margaret, wearing a silk coat covered with primroses with a matching yellow toque tilted forward on to her forehead with her hair brushed up over the brim at the back; the Duchess of Gloucester, in a pale pink grosgrain coat with mink collar and a hat of tiny curled ostrich feathers; the Princess Royal with the Earl and Countess of Harewood, and Lord Mountbatten. Then came Princess Marina with the Duchess of Kent and Prince Michael, and, as always, the bride's mother attracted the admiration of all those assembled in the ancient abbey. Her dress of gold tissue, worn over a slim sheath of silk richly embroidered with sparkling gold paillettes, was the most exotic to be seen there that day and her wide-brimmed cavalier-style hat, also covered with gold sequins, was adorned with a large diamond and pearl pendant brooch. The Duchess of Kent had chosen to wear a dress and coat of coral pink printed with a small design of white circles with a coolie-style hat to match of pink layered tulle. Queen Elizabeth the Queen Mother arrived, looking as graceful as ever in a wispy coat and dress of silver lace mounted on pale blue tulle – described as 'bluebell' – and to complete her ensemble had chosen a toning hat of osprey feathers. At last, to a fanfare of trumpets sounded by the trumpeters of the Royal Military School of Music, came Her Majesty the Queen, wearing pale green silk organza. The dress, with rounded neckline, was embroidered with a lily-of-the-valley motif worn under a plain see-through coat of sheer silk. The theme of lilies-of-the-valley was followed in the hat she wore, covered with thousands of these tiny flowers and veiled so lightly that the veiling was hardly noticeable. As the Queen made her way along the nave, accompanied by Prince Philip and the Prince of Wales, the bridal attendants arrived and stood under the long white awning at the west door to await Princess Alexandra's arrival. The five bridesmaids wore long dresses of pale cream ziberline, a fabric slightly heavier than silk though no longer manufactured today. They were designed with wide trumpet sleeves and full skirts and the bridesmaids wore bandeaux head-dresses of the same fabric. The two page-boys wore the kilt with white silk shirts and black patent shoes with wide silver buckles.

The bridegroom and his best man, Mr Peregrine Fairfax, were in their seats near

The Duchess of Kent (back to camera), Lady Moyra Hamilton and Princess Anne arrange the bride's voluminous train.

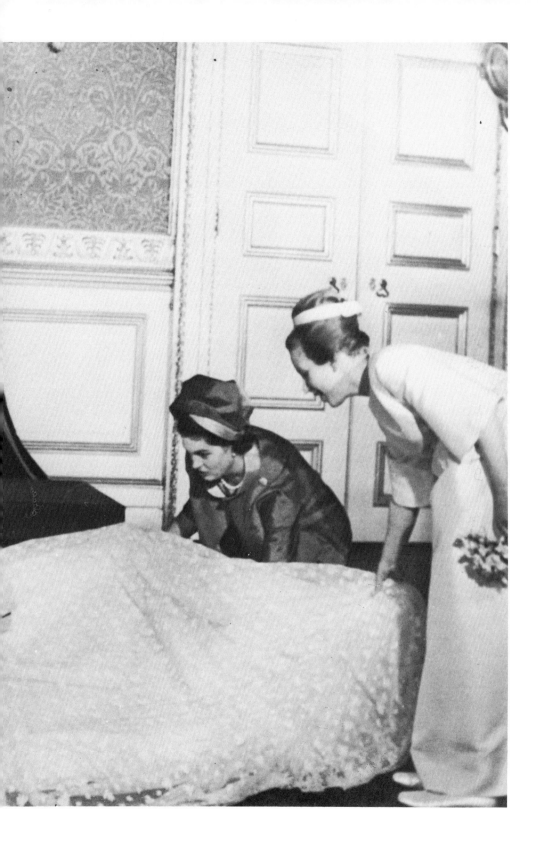

the choir stalls and the scene was now set for the arrival of the bride. The abbey, as one observer put it, looked just like Ascot; a riot of colour. On either side of the high altar huge urns were filled with massive displays of cherry blossom, guelder-roses, lilac, narcissi, hyacinths and rhododendrons. The chandeliers illuminated the splendid Persian carpets laid across the sacrarium and the uniforms of the Gentle-men-at-Arms added a welcome splash of scarlet to a vibrant, yet overall scene of pastel shades.

High above the altar in Henry v's chantry, the trumpeters rose. The bride was here. Slowly, as another fanfare filled the church, she made her way to the west door, a tall, graceful figure, looking very beautiful in her magnolia lace gown and veil, the lights catching the diamonds of her mother's tiara. She smiled at her brother and then as the organ and choir joined in the processional hymn, 'Holy, Holy, Holy, Lord God Almighty', Princess Alexandra, carrying a Victorian posy of freesias, narcissi, stephanotis and lilies-of-the-valley, began her walk down the long blue-carpeted nave. The weight of her voluminous train slowed her progress to a snail's pace. Behind came the attendants, linking hands and clearly remembering the lessons they had been taught during the rehearsals. Princess Marina leaned forward to watch her daughter approach, and Mr Ogilvy stepped forward.

The service followed the lines of Princess Marina's own wedding. After the Dean of Westminster had opened the ceremony with the familiar words, the Archbishop of Canterbury, Dr Michael Ramsay, conducting his first royal wedding since being appointed to that ancient office (he was formerly Archbishop of York) stepped forward to marry the couple. Psalm XXXVII was sung, followed by the anthem, 'God be in my head', and in the absence of an address, the Vicar of Kensington, the Rev. H. L. O. Rees, read the thirteenth chapter of the First Epistle of St Paul to the Corinthians. The wedding hymn, 'Love divine all loves excelling', followed and after the singing of the National Anthem the Princess and her husband made their way into the Chapel of St Edward the Confessor, to sign the marriage registers.

Finally, as another fanfare rang out, the bride and bridegroom appeared in the chapel doorway. The bride turned to Princess Anne and said, 'Your turn next', to which Anne looked surprised and exclaimed, 'Me?' The Receiver-General, Mr Reginald Pullen, wearing his bright red cassock and black academic gown, who had been watching the preceding procession of the clergy, advised the bride and bridegroom that it was now time for them to leave the chapel and, as the notes of the fanfare mellowed into those of Widor's *Toccata in F*, they crossed the broad sacrarium. Princess Alexandra curtsied to the Queen, her husband bowed.

Outside, the Glass Coach moved forward ready to take the Princess and her bridegroom back to St James's Palace and the wedding-breakfast which was to be attended by about seventy relations and friends. Once there, the couple personally greeted their guests, including members of their staff from both London and Scotland, then it was time to go upstairs to the crimson and gold throne room for the family photographs. There, Angus presented each of his wife's bridesmaids with a gold bracelet commemorating the occasion and the family helped arrange the Princess's magnificent train; Princess Margaret, a cigarette and her gloves in one hand, directed the small attendants to their places. An hour or so later in the picture gallery, filled with hundreds of red baccarat roses, the bride and bridegroom mounted the platform on which the wedding-cake was set and, brandishing a large silver knife, made the first incision. Angus, amid laughter, told his wife, 'Go on, now you do the lot,' before responding to the Duke of Kent's toast.

For a while longer the couple stayed at the reception mingling with their guests, the Princess's train being carried around by her lady-in-waiting, Moyra Hamilton, then it was time to slip next door to Clarence House to change into day clothes. Alexandra put on a wool suit of bright flamingo pink with a cream silk blouse and a turban hat of shantung silk, and the bridegroom changed into a more comfortable suit.

Below, in the Tudor yard of Friary Court, Princess Marina's limousine was waiting to drive the newly weds to Heathrow Airport where an aircraft of the Queen's Flight waited to fly them up to Scotland. Fog meant that the small plane had to be diverted to Lossiemouth where they were greeted by the commanding officer, Captain David Kirke, and his wife. After a long day in London, Princess Alexandra and Mr Ogilvy happily accepted Captain Kirke's offer of refreshments and in fact stayed with the couple at the commander's house for an hour and a half, watching the repeats of their wedding on television, before driving the eighty miles to the Queen Mother's estate, Birkhall. A fortnight later Alexandra and Angus were bound for Spain.

9

Changing Attitudes

For the Royal Family, the 1970s were to see changes unimagined just a quarter of a century ago. At last, the Queen and her family were being portrayed as human beings with a job to do rather more than as a group of highly privileged individuals whose rôles were somewhat ambiguous. From the rather remote images of, say, her grandparents, King George V and Queen Mary – who viewed their royal calling in much the same way as did Queen Victoria – Elizabeth II has emerged as a much warmer personality; a Queen with whom the vast percentage of the population can more easily identify, and a Head of State who, it cannot be denied, continues to work tirelessly in the best interests of her country. By the end of the 1960s, the Prince of Wales graduated from an academic youth and, with his sister, began to shoulder some of the burden of his family's official life.

There was also a timely change in attitude towards the question of marriage and, even more important in this day and age, towards the question of divorce.

In 1960 divorce for royalty was virtually unheard of, though Queen Victoria, rather surprisingly given her rigid belief in the sanctity of marriage, had sanctioned the divorce of her granddaughter, Princess Marie-Louise. But perhaps the circumstances seemed exceptional. Princess Marie-Louise recorded in her memoirs: 'As time went on, I became increasingly aware that my husband [Prince Aribert of Anhalt] and I were drifting farther and farther apart.... In fact, I was not wanted ... and from [an] enthusiastic girl of eighteen, I became a disillusioned woman.' Queen Victoria, aware of 'Louie's' unhappiness, sent a message: 'Send my granddaughter home to me.'

The 1970s saw three royal weddings, each in style a contradiction of the one before, and in 1978 the much-publicized, traumatic marriage of Princess Margaret and Lord Snowdon was finally dissolved. The Princess's divorce was pronounced on 24 May in the family division of the High Court along with some twenty other divorce cases which were heard in only 113 seconds. Another chapter was added to the modern history of the British monarchy.

Yet despite the more informal contact now established between monarchy and people, some members of the Royal Family remain comparatively unknown entities. To the public at large, the Gloucesters tend to be 'vague' royal figures. The reasons for this are straightforward enough, for the Gloucesters have never gone out of their

Birgitte van Deurs, Princess Richard of Gloucester, on her wedding day, 8 July 1972.

BELOW: Prince and Princess Richard of Gloucester seem unaware of the flurry of activity behind them as they prepare to leave St Andrew's Church, Barnwell, after their wedding. Princess Alice, Duchess of Gloucester, is about to straighten the bride's train while Prince William chats to local people.

way to court publicity and it is extremely doubtful that they will be remembered by history – one might even look upon them as 'supporting players' in the royal show.

Towards the end of his life, the Queen's uncle, Henry, Duke of Gloucester, faded completely from the public arena when ill-health confined him to the family's estate, Barnwell in Northamptonshire. In the meantime, his wife continued to carry out her duties in typically quiet fashion while their sons followed their own careers. Prince Richard was a full-time architect, and Prince William, in between overseas diplomatic postings, managed his father's business affairs at Barnwell.

Essentially they were a quiet, pleasant country family who helped to make the Queen's official life slightly less onerous by undertaking a fair amount of royal duties. Having established this point, it is easy to understand why Prince Richard, or as he is known today, the Duke of Gloucester, is still relatively unknown. As far as he was concerned, his blood link with the Queen – they are first cousins – placed him under no obligation to lead any other life than that of a private individual, working for a living. He had never received any form of official income, had never served in the armed forces thereby tying him to such formal engagements as regimental dinners and the like, and, in short, he had not been trained, unlike those closer to the throne, to expect a loftier royal office. His elder brother William, a likeable, healthy young man, would, in due course, succeed his father as Duke and presumably he would assume his own quota of royal engagements, while reviving his father's own links with a variety of charitable organizations. But in August 1972, three months after the death of another royal prince – the Duke of Windsor – and two years before the death of his father, Prince William was killed in a flying accident at a Midlands air show. He was thirty. Gradually, but reluctantly, Prince Richard, architect, photographer and author, was pushed more and more into the limelight until he himself succeeded to the dukedom of Gloucester in 1974.

By this time, Richard had a wife to help him overcome the blow that fate had dealt him. A nice-looking girl, she was Birgitte van Deurs, the daughter of a Danish lawyer. She and Richard had met at Cambridge as the result of a blind date, or more accurately, as the result of a meeting arranged between the Prince and another Danish girl. Birgitte went along as chaperone.

That initial meeting resulted in the announcement of Richard and Birgitte's engagement in the spring of 1972, followed by their wedding on 8 July that same year.

There were no plans for a lavish society wedding on this occasion chiefly because Prince Richard wanted to be married quietly; and indeed, in at least one respect his wedding could be compared with that of Princess Beatrice in July 1885. For both were celebrated in a country setting and both in unpretentious parish churches.

Prince Richard's wedding was solemnized in the village church of St Andrew, no more than two hundred yards from his home at Barnwell Manor, and his decision delighted the local people. At that time the village's oldest inhabitant, Mrs Florence

The bride and bridegroom shelter beneath a large umbrella as they make their way down the rain-soaked path.

Strickson, summed up the villagers' thoughts when she told newsmen, 'I thought he would get married in London or Windsor,' and then added, 'but it would not be right for me to question what royalty does – it's their business.'

On the day of the wedding, however, it seemed that royalty's business had once again become everybody's business. The streets of the small village with its population of 360, its limestone cottages, rambler roses and picturesque bridge spanning an idle brook, were overrun by tourists and visitors from neighbouring counties, as well as journalists from Fleet Street and television cameramen.

The wedding ceremony was set for four o'clock; the church decorated with pink and white roses and sweet peas – though in moderation because the best man, Prince William, suffered from hay-fever. Through the rain, which spoiled the original plan for the royal party to walk back from the church to the manor house, the ninety guests drawn from family and close friends, began to arrive. Queen Elizabeth the Queen Mother together with the Prince of Wales and Princess Margaret flew into Barnwell by royal helicopter to lunch with the bridegroom's mother, Princess Alice, Duchess of Gloucester; a little later the bride, who was also at the house with her parents and two half-sisters, went to her room to dress for the wedding. Norman Hartnell had created Princess Alice's wedding attire in 1935 and so it seemed fitting that her son's bride should also wear a Hartnell gown. His brief had been to design something suitable for a quiet country wedding. He had produced just that; a long dress of white Swiss organdie with a high neck and long sleeves on which was embossed a floral motif. Birgitte's white tulle veil, not quite floor-length, was edged, like Princess Margaret's in 1960, with white organdie piping and it was secured by the simplest band of creamy stephanotis, a favourite bridal flower. Princess Alice herself had made her daughter-in-law's bridal bouquet and, modelled on a traditional Danish wedding sheaf, it was composed of white and cream summer flowers bound with satin ribbon.

Shortly before four o'clock the royal party arrived at the church. Prince Michael of Kent escorted the tiny figure of Princess Alice, Countess of Athlone, at that time one of two surviving grandchildren of Queen Victoria, wearing a beige dress with a wide-brimmed flower-trimmed hat; the Prince of Wales with his grandmother dressed in turquoise blue; his aunt, Princess Margaret, dressed in a yellow and white polka-dot coat; and the groom's mother, wearing a white and navy dress under an off-white coat with a plain navy-blue straw hat to match.

There were no bridesmaids or pages at this wedding and so the next arrival, shielded by a huge umbrella, was the bride herself. For once the press were barred from entering the church since this was designated a *private* wedding in the strictest sense. The Dean of Windsor, assisted by the Rev. Peter Bustin, Vicar of Barnwell, married the couple – Birgitte Eva did not promise to 'obey' Richard Alexander Walter George, by the way – and little more than an hour later, it was time to return to Barnwell Manor and the wedding-reception. This too, was an informal affair with a buffet instead of the usual formal royal wedding-breakfast. It was at this point that the ailing Duke of Gloucester joined the party.

Society photographer Tom Hustler, who had taken pictures of Richard and Bir-gitte at the time of their engagement, was again invited to act as the official wedding photographer, and perhaps something he said afterwards will illustrate the down-to-earth nature of this particular royal marriage. When asked if anything in particular had stuck out in his mind he said: 'That I was allowed to be of so much help to the bride. Most photographers don't actually help the bride ... but here I found I wasn't an interloper, I was one of a team helping a wedding-day to go smoothly. I showed the bride the best way to hold her bouquet ... and I discussed with her the best way to hold her train.' But if he had any qualms about dealing with so many royal personalities, the Queen Mother, with characteristic ease, asked Mr Hustler, 'You must have photographed a great many weddings. Aren't the smaller ones so much nicer?' Certainly small gatherings on such occasions must be a refreshing change for members of the Royal Family, but for those closer to the throne, as was seen with Princess Anne's marriage the following year, small royal weddings aren't always possible. In any event, a good deal was to develop during the next twelve months and Anne's grand-scale wedding was to have something of a cheering effect on a gloomy political and national outlook.

A grim winter of industrial discontent faced Britain in November 1973, leading to a State of Emergency and the subsequent collapse of the Tory government. The stringent crisis proposals were unleashed on what was aptly but glibly called 'unlucky November 13'. It also happened to be the day before Princess Anne married Mark Phillips and, had some carping Labour MPs in the House of Commons had their way, the wedding wouldn't have taken place at all. It was hard to see how the cancella-tion of the Princess's big day would have helped relieve the country's congested lungs, however, and those who complained bitterly about wastage of fuel hadn't done their homework as thoroughly as they might. As one small example, petrol con-sumption on the day of the wedding would be cut to a minimum by the very fact that royal carriages – and the entire fleet was to be employed – rely on horsepower in the most basic sense, and those cars which would be used had been tanked up before the announcement of the Government's measures. Society's threatened de-privation of essential goods could not, therefore, be affected one way or another by the royal wedding and its cancellation would have been an extreme and unnecessary measure. Had the suggestion been taken seriously it would have been a highly un-popular move; for at this time, the often controversial Princess had reached the peak of her popularity.

Princess Anne has always been in the unfortunate position of putting people's backs up by an unguarded remark, her impatience with the press – magnified a hundred-fold in the following day's newspapers, of course – or her high-handed and often arrogantly brusque attitude. At the same time, her work, say, as President of the Save the Children Fund or as Patron of the Riding for the Disabled Association, tends to take a back seat, at least in the eyes of the press. Those directly concerned with what are referred to as 'the Princess Anne charities' highly commend her work and knowledge, but her attendance at an annual general meeting where she will speak publicly for an hour or so, without notes, is hardly newsworthy. Admittedly Princess Anne does little or nothing to improve her battered public image nowadays, but at the time of her wedding she had been behaving herself, and the press she received was generally complimentary.

All that aside, however, one thing was abundantly clear: her wedding had aroused incalculable interest, not only within the United Kingdom but abroad, with the result that over two hundred foreign journalists converged on London to cover the occasion. It was going to be a glittering affair which would vie in splendour with the marriage of her aunt – with whom temperamentally Anne had much in common – thirteen years before. Television coverage would be far wider, indeed unparalleled, and although the advent of colour television and the more sophisticated techniques of transmission promised to keep many more at home glued to their televisions, thousands of people were expected to flock into London for the atmosphere of the occasion if for nothing else. In any event, there was no reason at all why people shouldn't enjoy themselves, and early arrivals along the processional route were assured of a grandstand view of the royal bride and her family, because, as always, the Queen was no admirer of strict security. That wasn't to say there wouldn't be any, of course, and on the day itself, many plain-clothes detectives would mingle with the crowds of well-wishers; they would occupy places in tall buildings overlooking the procession's path to and from Westminster, armed with high-powered binoculars and high-velocity rifles; and they would conduct thorough searches of Westminster Abbey itself. The first team of police with tracker-dogs would make the first search at dawn. Since terrorism was fast becoming the scourge of the 1970s, the Commissioner of Police was leaving nothing to chance.

Princess Anne's engagement to the then Lieutenant Mark Phillips, Queen's Dragoon Guards – announced by Her Majesty on 29 May 1973 – followed weeks in which denial followed denial, and rumours of an impending marriage gathered momentum at every turn. The Buckingham Palace press office was inundated with calls from journalists. They were told there was no truth in the story and if the press office staff *suspected* that something was about to happen even they didn't know officially. This made the press office look very foolish in Fleet Street when the announcement was eventually made and their protests that 'we really didn't know' were met with many a raised eyebrow.

For now, however, the question that was being asked was, 'Who *is* Mark Phillips?' It had already been established that he had followed his father into the Dragoons and was a keen horseman and showjumper – he and Anne had been seen exercising their horses together on the now famous occasion when *he* simply kept his head down while *she* bounded over to tell the lurking press men to buzz off, or words to that effect. Princess Anne pointed out that they had first met in 1968 at a reception held for the British Olympic Equestrian team, but save for the rare mention of his name in one or other of the gossip columns, Mark was a completely unknown entity. In fact, few beyond the inner sanctum of Buckingham Palace had any idea that Anne had given up hopes of marrying Richard Meade, another member of the showjumping fraternity to whom she was supposed to have been secretly engaged. Another beau was Sandy Harper, a trendy polo-playing friend of Prince Charles, who was a close friend of Princess Anne.

Details of Mark Phillips' background were inevitably made public soon enough through the newspapers and through television features hastily compiled for transmission on the day of the royal engagement itself. Unfortunately, because the features were designed to inform the public at large they followed very predictable lines and the questions tended to be rather fatuous. Would Princess Anne's marriage to a commoner set a precedent for Prince Charles's eventual marriage was one question put to Hugo Vickers, an authority on the monarchy, when he was interviewed for Southern Television. A little more research would have revealed that an arranged marriage hasn't taken place within the Royal Family for some considerable time and, as this book has shown, princes and princesses have been marrying commoners for the best part of the twentieth century.

In the meantime, however, genealogists had been doing some research of their own and had come up with a complete, if unremarkable Phillips family tree. An overall examination of both parents' pedigrees revealed that a sixteenth-century nobleman had held office as Vice-Chamberlain of the first Queen Elizabeth's household and another, a godson of the same monarch, was responsible not only for writing poetry but also for improving Tudor hygiene by inventing the valve water closet. Less distinguished predecessors included a toll collector, a mining engineer, a hat finisher, a painter and decorator, one or two barristers, a warehouseman and several parsons – one of whom was chaplain to Victoria, Duchess of Kent, the mother of Queen Victoria. One all-important, if obscure link, with the Royal Family was found in Isabel Griffith, a twelfth-century gentlewoman who, it seems, was an ancestor of Queen Elizabeth the Queen Mother.

Hugo Vickers also pointed out to Southern Television viewers that Mark's maternal grandfather, Brigadier J.G. Tiarks, Colonel of the King's Dragoon Guards, was at one stage ADC to Princess Anne's maternal grandfather, King George VI, though this in itself was quite usual because high-ranking service personnel are often given such appointments.

Anne and Mark's wedding was set for Wednesday 14 November 1973, a day which was also the twenty-fifth birthday of Prince Charles. It was also barely a week before the twenty-sixth wedding anniversary of the Queen and Prince Philip. It seemed a rather long engagement – May to November – especially since most of the recent royal engagements have been followed within three or four months by the wedding itself. But there was much to arrange.

As the wedding-day approached, the press began disclosing information released by the palace, building up to a flood of souvenir editions and colour posters, special articles on both bride and bridegroom, interviews with those directly concerned with the arrangements and turning one or two molehills into mountains. The biggest of these erupted over the contribution private soldiers were asked to make towards a wedding-present for the Princess. 'Outrageous!' thundered those unaware that the *maximum* contribution requested was five pence. Once more Princess Anne was cast in an unbecoming light, but this time through no fault of her own; she simply wanted to get married with as little fuss and bother as possible. And, if she had to put up with the trappings of a full royal wedding, her instructions were brief: make it simple, cut the red tape to a minimum and dispense with some of the traditions adhered to for past occasions. Four apparent traditions that were dispensed with were the choice of designer for Anne's wedding-gown; the number of bridal attendants; the baker of the royal wedding-cake; and the foreign royal guests – *no* heads of state.

On the first count, Susan Small Limited and more particularly the company's design-director, Maureen Baker, had dressed the Queen's daughter for four or five years, more or less since she had started undertaking her own share of official royal engagements in 1968. It was to this smart, quietly efficient woman that Princess Anne had said, 'Of course you'll make my wedding-dress.' Dumbfounded, Mrs Baker exclaimed that she felt sure that she would be asked to help with the trousseau, 'but I was certain the dress itself would go to somebody like Hartnell'. But Princess Anne was not numbered among Sir Norman's royal clients and there seemed no reason why she should change her habits now.

The Princess's choice to be attended at her wedding by one bridesmaid and one page-boy was justified when she said candidly in a television interview, 'I know what it's like having yards of uncontrollable children.' In fact Anne had acted as bridesmaid at no fewer than six weddings and almost without exception there were always 'yards of uncontrollable children' in attendance. On 14 November, her bridesmaid would be her cousin Sarah, the nine-year-old daughter of Princess Margaret and Lord Snowdon, and the page-boy would be her nine-year-old brother, Edward.

After the near-controversy of the Army's monetary contribution towards her wedding-present, it fell to the Army Catering Corps to design and bake the cake; as tall as Anne herself, in four tiers, and weighing 145 lbs. This prized confection, the handiwork of Warrant-Officer David Dodd, was made from $12\frac{1}{2}$ lb of flour, 84 eggs, 16 lb of marzipan and two bottles of brandy. The break with tradition here was that royal wedding-cakes in the past have invariably been supplied by McVitie & Price or Lyons.

The fourth change concerning invitations to foreign royalty took the unprecedented form of excluding reigning monarchs – though Prince Rainier of Monaco and his wife were invited. Instead, the few remaining European royal houses were represented by a band of crown princes and princesses and their spouses. Norway would be represented by King Olav's son and heir, Crown Prince Harald and his attractive wife, the former Miss Sonja Haraldsen; the Netherlands sent Crown Princess Beatrix and her German-born husband, Prince Claus; and the future King and Queen of Spain, Juan Carlos and Princess Sophia, then known as the Prince and

ABOVE: Food for thought: three House of Commons chefs watch the royal procession drive to Westminster Abbey for the wedding of Princess Anne and Captain Mark Phillips on 14 November 1973.

BELOW: The bride takes her vows.

Princess of the Asturias, would be present with Sophia's brother, the exiled King Constantine of Greece and his Danish wife Anne-Marie, the youngest sister of the present Queen of Denmark.

The 'letters to the editor' pages of the popular press appeared to yield a variety of reactions to the forthcoming event. Most people seemed to want to express publicly their good wishes for the couple's future though others saw it as an opportunity to criticize the extraordinary amount of publicity surrounding Anne and Mark and to complain bitterly about the smart Georgian house they would move into at Sandhurst for the unspeakably low rent of £8 per week. The publicity was understandable, the allocation of Oak Grove House wasn't – especially since rented accommodation anywhere was fast becoming a nightmare for innumerable people, young and old alike. Few people envisaged further promotion for Mark – he had recently been elevated from the rank of Lieutenant to that of Captain – but those who thought they saw it coming made themselves heard in good time. As it was, the Princess's husband-to-be wasn't given his field-marshal's baton and those who also anticipated his further elevation to the peerage, perhaps as an earl like Princess Margaret's husband, were disappointed – at least for the first few years of their married life; even now there seems to be no rush to make Captain Mark Phillips' name ring to the sound of further glory.

For once in their lives, however, Anne and Mark were given a chance to speak for themselves and, in a carefully worded way, to answer some of their critics. The occasion was the recording of a ninety-minute television interview due to be transmitted on the eve of the wedding. Lights, cameras and videotape machines were set up in Princess Anne's own sitting-room, overlooking the courtyard of Buckingham Palace, and while the sound of a Guards band wafted up through the windows, the Princess and her fiancé faced both BBC and Independent Television interviewers.

On the subject of Oak Grove House, Mark was the first to speak. 'There has been a lot in the press about it,' he began, but 'if a married officer goes to Sandhurst as an instructor, he is given quarters; that is the normal practice. ... People have said £8 a week is very cheap, but I am paying the going Army rate for a house, which is at a colonel's rate, paid out of my captain's salary.' It could have been argued by the pedantic that Oak Grove was therefore a colonel's dwelling but before anybody even dared consider splitting hairs with Princess Anne (who is an honorary colonel) on the subject, she went on to reply to a question about the criticism levelled at them from certain quarters, especially about the use of the Royal Yacht *Britannia* for their Caribbean honeymoon, and the expense of the wedding: 'The answer to the wedding is that it is none of our business. The honeymoon in *Britannia* is quite simple. The half-truths about that are numerous, but the yacht is on her way to New Zealand for the Queen, and has to pass through the West Indies to get there.' But how had the criticism affected them? the interviewers persisted. 'It is distressing,' said the Princess, 'because it is not accurate and it puts the blame at our feet when we don't really think it has anything to do with us.' Then Anne took up the point of suitable housing once again. 'This myth that we could have had another house and we were just being plain difficult about Sandhurst was another very irritating criticism because it was misinformed.'

Finally, on the subject of the press, the Princess was asked why at times she seemed to have lost patience with photographers during her equestrian events. She smiled and glanced at Mark, and explained carefully:

I accept all the press when on an official engagement as part of the scenery, but at horse trials the 'me' that does the official duties couldn't possibly ride a horse. It's a different sort of 'me'. I have to concentrate on what I am doing. I can't think about where the press are and things like that. If I appear to lose my patience, I would appear to lose my patience with anybody who perhaps got in the way.

By dawn the following day, 14 November, spectators had been in place for hours. Many arrived soon after midnight and were joined by others who had either gone home for dinner and a rest, or had decided to stay in town and take in a film or a show. In any event, by the time the bitter, wet night had turned into a brilliant sunlit morning an estimated crowd of 47,000 were lining the route; an impressive number given that it was winter and most people preferred the convenience of switching on their televisions, and that a national holiday hadn't been declared in celebration.

Excitement began to run high with the sight of the troops shortly after nine o'clock. A detachment of the 10th Princess Mary's Own Gurkha Rifles marched along the Mall and were followed shortly by the bands. That of the Coldstream Guards positioned itself at the junction of Marlborough Road and the Mall, the band of the Scots Guards was further along at the foot of the Duke of York's Steps; the 3rd Battalion the Light Infantry on Horse Guards Parade, the band of the Royal Air Force at Whitehall Gardens, and the band of the Royal Marines in Parliament Square. To their commanding officers had been issued the brief concerning salutes, or 'compliments' as they are known. To Her Majesty the Queen's procession, the order went out, Royal salute, lower colours, National Anthem in full. To His Royal Highness the Duke of Edinburgh proceeding to Westminster Abbey with Her Royal Highness the Bride, Royal salute, lower colours, National Anthem in full. 'Bands will start playing in the case of the Queen's processions, when the outriders of the carriage are twenty paces from the band's near flank. In the case of Her Royal Highness the Bride's procession when the leading division of the Captain's Escort is ten paces from the band's near flank.'

Major R.A.G. Courage of London District Headquarters, the co-ordinator of the wedding's military aspect, said that in general a royal wedding on the scale of Princess Anne's was easier to organize than a state occasion because fewer troops were involved. But on 14 November, an overwhelming number were in evidence. Drawn from the Army, the Navy and the Royal Air Force, 845 troopers and 43 officers would be on parade, including a detachment from the bridegroom's regiment, the 1st the Queen's Dragoon Guards. Quite apart from these there were detachments from Princess Anne's regiments (the 14th/20th King's Hussars, Worcestershire and

Princess Anne hands her bridal bouquet to Lady Sarah Armstrong-Jones at the steps of the sacrarium, watched by the Duke of Edinburgh, Prince Edward, the bridegroom and the best man, Captain Eric Grounds.

Sherwood Foresters Regiment and the 8th Canadian Hussars (Princess Louise's)), who were to form the guard of honour at Westminster Abbey; the sixteen trumpeters, who would sound the fanfares and accompany the hymn-singing in the abbey, and the Sovereign's and Captain's Escorts of the Household Cavalry, composed of the Life Guards and the Blues and Royals.

Little more than an hour after the troops had lined the streets, the crowds near Buckingham Palace itself saw the fleet of royal carriages drive into the courtyard and disappear through the central arch ready to collect the members of the Royal Family. The family were assembling in the Queen's private suite, overlooking Constitution Hill, down which, with the sun glinting on their helmets and breastplates, giving the illusion of a thousand and more mirrors, rode the Household Cavalry, from their barracks at Knightsbridge. The scene, like so many more that day, seemed as though it was plucked from the realms of make-believe and, despite the gloomy economic picture, every Briton there that day felt an unexpected pang of patriotism; the more so as the Queen's procession swung out of the palace gates at eleven o'clock to the sound of the National Anthem, the roar of the crowd and the clatter of the Sovereign's Escort.

'This has made our holiday, we're just so lucky,' was heard all round in many accents, and one was inclined to nod sympathetically as one Danish visitor, slightly over-awed by it all, said, 'We have nothing like this now in Denmark.' Indeed, one was made aware that Britain, for so long the real expert at such things as royal ceremonial, had triumphed yet again to the delight of thousands, and all the petty complaints that had consumed so much news space faded away without a second thought when caught up in the general euphoria of what undeniably was a very happy occasion.

In the picturesque Scottish State Coach, with its large windows and transparent roof surmounted by a scarlet and gold crown, the Queen, dressed in sapphire blue silk (and as Hartnell liked to see her, 'in one colour, hat to hem'), drove to her daughter's wedding accompanied by the Queen Mother in beige and gold, and Princes Andrew and Edward. In fact, as many remarked, the Queen's youthful appearance belied her forty-seven years, and though she is not very photogenic, this was one of the occasions on which the cameras successfully managed to catch not so much an official side to the sovereign's nature, as that of a proud and delighted mother.

During the twelve minutes that separated Her Majesty's departure from Buckingham Palace, with the remaining members of her family following, the exuberance of those waiting in the streets reached bursting point and it was to a cacophony of sound that Princess Anne drove from her home in the Glass Coach. At first sight of the carriage as it passed from the inner quadrangle to the courtyard, those massed behind the impassive marble gaze of Queen Victoria seated, larger than life, on the memorial erected to her in front of the palace, cheered wildly; the sound all but drowning the band which had struck up the National Anthem. This was the reception Anne received all along the wedding route.

19 73. Marriage solemnized at *Westminster Abbey* in the *Close* of *St Peter: Westminster* in the County of *London*

No.	When Married.	Name and Surname.	Age.	Condition.	Rank or Profession.	Residence at the time of Marriage.	Father's Name and Surname.	Rank or Profession of Father.
20	14th November 1973	Mark Anthony Peter Phillips	25	Bachelor	Captain: 1st The Queens Dragoon Guards	Mount House, Great Somerford Chippenham, Wiltshire.	Peter William Garside Phillips	Major: M.C Company Director
		Anne Elizabeth Alice Louise Mountbatten-Windsor	23	Spinster	Princess of the United Kingdom of Great Britain and Northern Ireland	Buckingham Palace	His Royal Highness The Prince Philip.	Duke of Edinburgh K.G. O.M.

Married in *Westminster Abbey* according to the Rites and Ceremonies of the *Established Church* by *Special Licence* by

this Marriage was solemnized between us, { *Mark Phillips* / *Anne* }

+ *Michael Cantuar*

Eric S Abbot Dean

In the presence of us :—

Elizabeth R

Philip

Anne Phillips

Alice Page *Peter Phillips*

Edward

Sarah Phillips

Eric Grounds

Elizabeth R

Margaret *Alexandra* *Michael*

Alice

Charles

Andrew

Angus Ogilvy

Snowdon

Richard

Sarah

Mountbatten of Burma

Birgitte

Edward

Linley

George St Andrews. *Helen Windsor.*

ABOVE: The Westminster Abbey register recording the marriage of Princess Anne and Captain Mark Phillips.

BELOW: Prince Edward straightens his sister's long train as she curtsies to the Queen at the conclusion of the marriage service.

ABOVE: A pensive moment for the royal bride as she and her husband drive back to Buckingham Palace in the Glass Coach.

BELOW: Princess Anne and Mark Phillips on the balcony of Buckingham Palace, acknowledging the cheers from below.

From her place in the abbey – this time high above the altar – Audrey Russell had begun her description of the scene. The Royal Family had arrived and had taken their seats in the sacrarium. Already the pattern of vibrant, glowing colours had built up; the bright blue carpet stretching away to the great west door, past the tomb of the Unknown Warrior surrounded by bright red poppies, the magnificent crystal chandeliers ablaze, the robes of the clergy, the soldiers and the gentlemen-at-arms and the outfits of the royal ladies. The Queen's outfit contrasted well with that of her mother's, banded in the Queen Mother's own inimitable style with sable, and it blended with the aquamarine coat and hat chosen by Princess Alice, Duchess of Gloucester, the pale lilac outfit of the doyenne of the Royal House of Windsor, Princess Alice, Countess of Athlone (then nearing her ninety-first birthday), the sea-green velvet redingote of Princess Alexandra, Princess Richard's coat scattered with scarlet poppies, and the Duchess of Kent's velvet redingote of amber and ochre. Princess Margaret had shopped at Dior of London for her gold and brown outfit, and then there were the foreign royal ladies. Crown Princess Sonja of Norway in bright turquoise blue, Princess Sophia of Spain in cream with a dark mink coat, and Princess Grace of Monaco who surprised most people by arriving in a white woollen coat with a white mink beret to match. 'It simply *isn't* done,' murmured fashion authorities, 'for anybody but the bride to wear white.' But there it was. If the Princess intended to cause a minor stir she had achieved her objective.

Then, at a little before 11.30a.m., the trumpeters stood in readiness to sound a flourish announcing Princess Anne's arrival. It caused a momentary scare for Audrey Russell who hadn't, so far, mentioned the bridegroom, in his newly designed full-dress uniform of the Dragoon Guards, yet on her monitor screen was seeing the bride descending from the Glass Coach. 'I knew he was there, of course,' she said afterwards, 'because I had seen him. But I couldn't go straight into describing Princess Anne's arrival until I had said something about Mark.' What had happened in fact, was that the bridegroom, together with his best man, Captain Eric Grounds, had stood back against a pillar to allow one or two aged clergy to pass slowly by. Then they came into view as they approached to take their seats in the lantern, at the foot of the steps to the sacrarium.

The fanfare rang through the abbey, the choir and the congregation stood, and Princess Anne appeared in her stunning wedding-dress, framed by the great west door through which countless princes and statesmen had passed during the abbey's nine hundred years of existence.

Waiting under the awning to see the bride make her entrance was Maureen Baker who, with the help of her assistant, had created the gown that chain-stores hastily, but poorly, tried to copy. The first imitation was on sale in the shops within hours, together with the tempting slogan, aimed at other brides-to-be, 'feel like a princess'. Nothing could compete with the original, however. 'A chain-store couldn't possibly do it,' said Maureen Baker. 'As an example, the bodice of Princess Anne's gown was cut in one with the skirt. There were no seams.' Nor could a moderately priced store afford the pearls and the mirror jewels which had gone into decorating the

Princess's gown and certainly they would never be able to use the same material. This had been specially woven to Maureen Baker's own specifications, using over one thousand threads of twenty denier silk in every inch. The Suffolk firm of Stephen Walters & Sons, who had been making fine silk for eight generations, were responsible for producing the fabric which the designer called Soie Annello. Tudor portraits had inspired the design and Mrs Baker had submitted altogether three sketches to Princess Anne.

Many years before, the Princess had said that she would like to be a traditional bride; at Westminster Abbey that day she had her wish. Her wedding-dress, of pure ivory colour, followed the traditional princess line. The moulded bodice, enhanced by graduated pin tucks, flared slightly into a semi-full skirt which flowed out behind her into a sweeping semi-circular train. The long sleeves were set over finely pleated under-sleeves of ivory chiffon edged with pearls, which fell gracefully away to form a point. Across the shoulders were a subtle reminder that this was as much a military wedding as a royal occasion and epaulettes had been picked out in tiny pearls, from which flowed a fine silk Court train reminiscent of the Queen's own bridal train, fastened with tiny silk-covered buttons. The embroidery was worked with silver, seed pearls and small mirror-jewels.

Princess Anne's hairdresser had created a style which looked slightly Edwardian and on it she wore the diamond fringe tiara, modelled on a Russian peasant head-dress, which had been loaned to the Princess by her grandmother. From it fell a long, misty veil of pure white silk tulle. To complete the picture, Anne carried a bouquet composed of fifteen white 'Jack Frost' roses, orchid stems from Singapore, stephanotis, lily-of-the-valley leaves and a sprig of myrtle, grown at Cowes on the Isle of Wight from a piece taken from Queen Victoria's bridal bouquet.

Behind the bride stood her two attendants. Young Prince Edward was dressed in a kilt, together with a black velvet jacket, silk shirt and lace jabot, and Lady Sarah Armstrong-Jones wore a long white pinafore dress over a blouse with small ruffled collar of white silk ribbon lattice-work, worked with five thousand seed pearls. With it, she wore a matching Juliet cap, and instead of a posy, carried a ball of white carnation petals.

The choir began to sing the processional hymn, 'Glorious things of thee are spoken'. The Dean of Westminster approached the bride and her father. 'Ma'am,' he asked, 'are you ready?' Princess Anne nodded and, smiling broadly, she took her father's arm for the four-minute walk along the nave.

It had been thirteen years since she had first stepped into Westminster Abbey for a royal wedding and on that occasion, Princess Margaret, the bride, had hardly responded to the light-hearted quips of Prince Philip. Now the Prince walked with his own daughter who, if she was even remotely nervous, didn't show it, and it seemed as they moved between the rows of guests, as if there was a good deal of private joke-swapping going on. Both the bride and her father grinned broadly and Philip obviously had none of King George VI's cares that 'everything would be all right'.

A happy study of Princess Anne and Mark Phillips following their wedding.

As the last notes of the hymn faded away, the Dean of Westminster stepped forward to open the marriage service. The Archbishop of Canterbury performed the actual wedding, and in the vows, Princess Anne promised to 'obey' her husband. Before the blessing the Archbishop addressed the congregation with the words, 'For as much as Mark Anthony Peter and Anne Elizabeth Alice Louise have consented together in holy wedlock, and have witnessed the same before God and this company, and thereto have given and pledged their troth either to other, and have declared the same by giving and receiving of a ring, and by joining of hands; I pronounce that they be man and wife together.'

The Princess and her bridegroom moved towards the high altar, while the choir sang Psalm XXIII, and the Precentor of the Abbey took up his position to intone the Lord's Prayer, followed by the Queen's cousin, the Rev. and Hon. Andrew Elphinstone, who had been specially invited to take part in the marriage ceremony.

The service moved to its close on a more musical note with the singing of the anthem, 'God be in my head'; the hymn, 'Immortal, invisible, God only wise'; and the National Anthem. During the time it took to sign the royal and abbey registers in the Chapel of St Edward the Confessor (the Princess being described as 'Anne Mountbatten-Windsor' in accordance with her mother's decree of February 1960), the choir sang two further anthems; Ralph Vaughan Williams' 'Let all the world in every corner sing' and Handel's superb composition 'Let their celestial concerts all unite'.

Then a final flourish, sounded by the trumpeters of the Dragoons, filled the abbey; Anne and Mark appeared in the narrow doorway of the chapel, crossed the sacrarium, honouring the Queen as they passed, and made their way back along the nave to Widor's *Toccata in F*, which has become something of a set piece at the close of royal wedding ceremonies. The bride and bridegroom approached the great west door, the Princess's veil billowing in a sudden cold draught, and for a moment they paused to exchange a word or two with a group of Captain Phillips' fellow officers. They went out to their waiting carriage, the acclaim of the crowds and the sound of the abbey's pealing bells.

Ninety minutes after the ceremony had begun, Princess Anne, Mrs Mark Phillips and her husband stepped out on to the balcony of Buckingham Palace to acknowledge the cheers from the crowds below. The Queen and Prince Philip joined them, as did Prince Charles who was urged by his sister to take a bow in thanks for the additional cries of 'Happy Birthday, Charlie'. Then it was time for the royal party to rejoin their guests – 130 had been invited to the now private celebration of the marriage – and to sit down at the small circular tables in the Ball-Supper Room where the wedding-breakfast was served. On the menu was egg, lobster, shrimps and tomato bound in light mayonnaise; partridge with button mushrooms, onions and bacon rolls; and peppermint bombe with grated chocolate inside, all of which was enjoyed with wines from the royal cellars, including Niersteiner 1969, Château Mouton Rothschild 1955 and Heidsieck Dry 1966.

Princess Anne and Mark's departure for the Caribbean was not scheduled until the following day, when, aboard Boeing 707 Zulu Foxtrot – a normal scheduled flight – they would leave London's Heathrow Airport *en route* to join the *Britannia*. What to do after the wedding-breakfast presented no problems, however, and the crowds who were still massed beyond the palace gates were not to be deprived of another look at the bridal pair. After a day in which they were beyond doubt the cynosure of all eyes, the only thing Anne and Mark wanted was a little peace and quiet and a place in the country where they could enjoy a light supper on their own and settle down. The ideal solution was Thatched House Lodge in Richmond Park, the home of Princess Alexandra and Angus Ogilvy. The Ogilvys suggested it, and Anne and Mark accepted. It was as isolated as possible – especially in winter when sightseers thought twice about loitering, and it was fairly close to Heathrow. The destination would be kept secret and it had been arranged that from Buckingham Palace the bride and groom would drive to a convenient spot – in this case the Royal Hospital, Chelsea – in an open landau and then change their mode of transport to speed in one of the Queen's state cars to Richmond.

So, at four o'clock, in the gathering dusk of that November evening, Princess Anne, now wearing a sapphire blue velvet coat – the shade having been matched with the sapphire in her engagement ring – with a wide mink collar and a matching white mink pill-box hat complete with pom-pom, left the palace in one of the semi-state landaus with her husband, escorted by a travelling party of the Household Cavalry. The crowds cheered, wished them both luck and threw handfuls of confetti after them and, as the small procession went on its way, still more people rushed out into the street from their offices or stood on balconies to watch them pass.

The following morning, as the couple started out for their honeymoon, they found the drive to Thatched House Lodge lined with cheering schoolchildren. Once at the airport, however, they boarded their aircraft, changed into more comfortable clothes and settled down to watch the in-flight film *Bequest to the Nation*. Their first stop was Barbados, followed by a leisurely cruise in *Britannia*. Then it was back to work on an official two-week tour of Ecuador, Columbia, Jamaica, Montserrat and Antigua, before returning to London on 17 December and, after all the sunshine, the remainder of a bleak winter.

One of the most intriguing marriages in the Queen's family – and the last to occur during the 1970s – took place five years after that of Princess Anne. The couple involved this time were Her Majesty's cousin, Prince Michael of Kent – younger brother of the Duke of Kent and a major in the Royal Hussars, currently working with the Intelligence Directorate of the Ministry of Defence – and the Bohemian-born Baroness Marie-Christine von Reibnitz, an interior designer with her own business based in London.

Three factors made this particular marriage more newsworthy than some. The first was the couple's mutual descent through eleven generations from Moritz, Land-grave of Hesse-Cassel and his consort, Countess Juliana of Nassau-Siegen; and through ten generations from Prince Ferdinand August of Lobkowicz, who married first Princess Claudia of Nassau (Marie-Christine's ancestor) and secondly Margravine Maria Anna of Baden (Prince Michael's ancestor).

The second and most controversial factor centred round the question of religion. Marie-Christine was and still is a Roman Catholic, and by the Act of Settlement of 1701, any member of the Royal Family marrying a Catholic forfeits the right of succession.

Thirdly, the 33-year-old baroness was a divorcee. Her first marriage to a merchant banker, Thomas Troubridge, had been annulled by the Roman Catholic church courts in August 1977, five years after she and Prince Michael had met at a shooting party at Barnwell Manor given by Princess Alice, Duchess of Gloucester.

Tom Troubridge, like Prince Michael, had been educated at Eton, but during the time that he and Marie-Christine were married Prince Michael was never more than an acquaintance. When the marriage ended, however, and Prince Michael eventually met Marie-Christine again, a romance ensued.

Under the circumstances marriage could not be a straightforward matter and, although the annulment had been granted, for Marie-Christine to marry Prince Michael in a Catholic church, as was her wish, it was necessary for Prince Michael to obtain a dispensation from the Pope himself. The couple had been given verbal assurance that this would be granted by the Apostolic Delegate, who had been in touch with the Vatican about the situation some months before the engagement was announced. It was for this reason that all the preparations for a church wedding in Vienna went ahead. It came as a great disappointment, then, just two weeks before the wedding, when the dispensation for Prince Michael was not granted.

The general public view was that the Pope's refusal was based on a statement, issued on behalf of Prince Michael at the time of his engagement, that any children of the marriage would be raised in the Anglican faith, although every effort would be made to ensure that they had a full understanding of their mother's religion. Prince Michael's announcement had not been designed to worsen an already uncomfortable situation but had been made innocently enough by the Prince speaking as an Anglican. It was also believed that the Privy Council would not have given their necessary approval to this royal marriage without Prince Michael's assurance that his children would be raised as Anglicans.

The Vatican's response that it would not recognize any union between Marie-Christine and Prince Michael wounded Marie-Christine deeply and a short time afterwards Prince Charles (whose name had been recently linked with that of a Catholic girl, hotly tipped as the future Princess of Wales, Marie-Astrid of Luxembourg) was caught up in something of a controversy over a speech he made about Church dogma in general. In the speech Prince Charles spoke of the unnecessary distress caused to couples when caught in a religious conflict. Most people took this as a thinly-veiled reference to the marriage of his kinsman, and clergy threw up their hands in furious indignation with the result that the reaction made headlines across the country and continued to simmer for several weeks.

The bride and bridegroom open the wedding ball with a Strauss waltz.

Nonetheless, church wedding or no church wedding, the couple would be married. Marie-Christine had always wanted to be married in her native Austria and now sadly abandoned the plans for a church wedding with a sung mass by the famous Vienna Boys' Choir, and substituted a private mass in a side-chapel to be attended only by the immediate family. Under the Marriages Act of 1949, no provision was made for a member of the Royal Family to be married in a British Registry Office. So now instead of the original plan to marry in the family parish church where her grandparents had been married, the customary compulsory civil ceremony would have to suffice – at least for the moment. Privately, Marie-Christine did not rule out the hope of a church wedding at some future date.

The marriage itself was a flurry of activity. The bridal couple flew out to Vienna on 27 June 1978 – three days before the wedding – and those members of the Royal Family who were to attend the ceremony joined them on 30 June. The press were at pains to stress that the presence of both Princess Anne and the late Lord Mountbatten proved that the Queen was delighted at her cousin's marriage, though the reports overlooked the more important consideration that the Queen had specifically approved the style and title of Royal Highness for her cousin's wife.

On the day of the ceremony a small crowd, intrigued by an English royal wedding taking place in the old Habsburg capital, gathered outside the town hall. After a family lunch Princess Anne arrived with Princess Alexandra and the rest of the royal guests and made their way up the 125 steps to the top-floor marriage chamber where thirty relatives were already assembled.

The bride arrived at three o'clock. She stepped from her limousine, paused briefly so that the press could get their pictures, and went inside. Her outfit, designed for this ceremony by Hardy Amies, was a simple suit of cream silk. The fitted jacket, fastened with a single button and tie belt, and the skirt with side pockets and soft gathers round the waist, were worn with a matching cream silk blouse with a tie neck. The baroness wore her hair in a fashion now known as the 'Princess Michael' style and it was decorated with two large pale cream gardenias.

When the party was gathered in the panelled antechamber it was discovered that both Prince Michael and his bride had forgotten their papers of identification – required to be presented under Austrian law – and while the ceremony went ahead, the Prince's private secretary, Sir Peter Scott, dashed back to the British Embassy to collect the all-important documents. Twenty minutes later the new Princess Michael of Kent reappeared, this time on the arm of her beaming husband, to pose for more photographs in an infectiously happy way.

Early that evening the newly-married pair met the press and television for more formal photographs on the lawns of the British Embassy, giving the Princess an opportunity to wear the Edwardian-style dress of cream silk and lace originally designed by Belleville-Sassoon for the church wedding. As she was leaving for the Embassy, however, Princess Michael tore the hem climbing into the car; unperturbed, she asked for needle and thread and repaired it during the drive. To complement her romantic dress the Princess wore her wedding present from her

ABOVE: Baroness Marie-Christine
von Reibnitz, flanked by her
mother, Countess Kockorowska
(left) and Princess Paul of
Yugoslavia (right), sets out for her
wedding at Vienna Town Hall,
30 June 1978.

At the formal British Embassy
reception following the church
blessing, the royal bride chats with
Princess Anne and the late Lord
Mountbatten.

husband, the diamond fringe tiara worn by both Princess Marina and Princess Alexandra at their weddings. This time a few stephanotis were scattered in her hair.

Then followed the main celebration of the day, a wedding ball or *brautsoiree* held in the grand Schwarzenburg Palace, which had been loaned by Princess Michael's cousin, Prince Karl zu Schwarzenburg. The party, organized by Patrick Lichfield's sister, Lady Elizabeth Shakerley, was a white tie and tiara affair. Following dinner, the hundred guests assembled on the terrace to watch a short ballet performed on the spot-lit lawns, and at the end of this the orchestra struck up a waltz in the grand chandelier-lit ballroom as bride and groom led their guests in a night of dancing. At midnight the lights went out and a huge candlelit buffet was wheeled in laden with dozens of magical castles in coloured sorbets and fruits.

It was obvious from the start that Princess Michael of Kent was about to establish for herself something of a unique reputation as a member of the British Royal Family. Even so, this popular royal marriage was inevitably compared with another which had not met with the establishment's unconditional approval, that of the Duke and Duchess of Windsor in 1937. The similarities between the two events were few, though the press still attempted to echo the attitudes taken at that time. For example, although Wallis Simpson may have been a divorcee she wasn't a Roman Catholic nor was she created a Royal Highness; Prince Michael (then sixteenth in line to the throne) may have had to forfeit his right of succession but he wasn't a king; the Windsors had, admittedly, taken part in a brief civil ceremony but it was immediately followed by a religious service. Prince and Princess Michael had to make do with a private mass in the small flower-filled, but otherwise stark, Schottenstift Chapel the following day.

This was followed by a splendid luncheon for a hundred guests at the British Embassy where the Duke of Kent, as best man, toasted the couple, speeches were made and the cake was cut. Forgetting the traumatic years through which they had passed to reach their happiness, the bridal couple flew off for their honeymoon in India and Iran.

On their return to London the Archbishop of Canterbury held a service of blessing for the couple at Lambeth Palace and this was followed by a reception at St James's Palace for a thousand guests which was attended by the entire Royal Family.

Princess Anne's wedding hadn't set a precedent for the marriage of royal figures to commoners, but perhaps, as the Royal Family embraced its first Roman Catholic princess for some three hundred years, the wedding of Prince and Princess Michael of Kent helped to introduce a new level of understanding towards the weddings of the royal house of Windsor.

RIGHT: Forbidden a church wedding by the Pope, Prince and Princess Michael of Kent were allowed a church blessing on the day after their civil marriage. The bride and bridegroom are seen arriving at the church.

BELOW: The wedding group in the garden of the British Embassy. Standing (left to right): Baron Friedrich von Reibnitz, the bride's brother; Count Laszlo Szapary, the bride's uncle; the Hon. Angus Ogilvy; Baron Gunther von Reibnitz, the bride's father; Princess Anne; Lady Helen Windsor, holding the bridal bouquet; Earl Mountbatten of Burma; Princess Alexandra and the Duke of Kent.

Index

Select Bibliography

HELEN CATHCART *Anne and the Princesses Royal* (W.H. Allen, 1973)
FRANCES DONALDSON *Edward VIII* (Weidenfeld and Nicolson, 1974)
DAVID DUFF *Hessian Tapestry* (Frederick Muller, 1967)
GRACE ELLISON *Life Story of Princess Marina* (Heinemann, 1934)
CHARLES GREVILLE *Journal of the Reign of Queen Victoria 1837–1852* (Longmans & Co)
ROBERT RHODES JAMES (Ed.) *Chips, The Diaries of Sir Henry Channon* (Weidenfeld and Nicolson, 1967)
ELIZABETH LONGFORD *Victoria R.I.* (Weidenfeld & Nicolson, 1964)
PRINCESS MARIE-LOUISE *Memories of Six Reigns* (Evans Brothers, 1956)
CHRISTOPHER WARWICK *The Royal Brides* (Leslie Frewin, 1975)
    The Illustrated London News (1919–47)
    The Sketch (July 1893)